Local Welfare and the Organization of
Social Services

Pietro Previtali • Eugenio Salvati

Local Welfare and the Organization of Social Services

Local Area Planning in the Lombardy Region

 Springer

Pietro Previtali
Department of Economics and Management
University of Pavia
Pavia, Italy

Eugenio Salvati
Department of Economics and Management
University of Pavia
Pavia, Italy

ISBN 978-3-030-66127-4   ISBN 978-3-030-66128-1   (eBook)
https://doi.org/10.1007/978-3-030-66128-1

This Springer imprint is published by the registered company Springer Nature Switzerland AG
The registered company address is: Gewerbestrasse 11, 6330 Cham, Switzerland

Contents

Chapter 1
Introduction

Abstract During the last years, the systems of local welfare are undergoing several organizational changes, which aim to redefine the relationship between the service's planner, providers and citizens and, consequently, between the social needs and the policy answer delivered. The book aims to provide valuable insights into the evolution of local welfare and the territorial organisation of social services by analysing the evolution of a specific organisational instrument, the Local Area Plan, which lies at the intersection between the themes of (sub) regional governance and models for the supply of to supply social services. The research will show how these peculiar governance arrangements to Italian local welfare have changed profoundly over time, becoming both a catalyst for policies planned at different levels and a reference point for all the territorial actors involved in social policies.

Keywords Local welfare · Public services' organization · Local area plan · Social policies · Multilevel governance

In these hard and complex times, the emergence of new social risks and changes in the socio-economic structure of our societies means that the welfare state is facing new challenges. Of particular note is the pressure exerted by new budgetary constraints and the consequential reduction in available resources. In a nutshell, welfare systems – both at a national and local level – need to reinvent themselves. New and more innovative services, better able to cope with social demands, are needed, and major efforts deployed to define new and more effective organisational structures in the governance of social assistance. This quest for reform can be seen as an unavoidable need forced on the field by the structural changes that are exerting pressure on state welfare systems.

In this context, the local level has acquired even more importance due to its direct proximity to citizens and their welfare needs. It is to the local level, also from the perspective of multilevel governance (Kazepov 2010), that new tasks, duties and powers have shifted, creating the impellent necessity to define new models and instruments better able to connect the multiplicity of actors involved in the produc-

P. Previtali, E. Salvati, *Local Welfare and the Organization of Social Services*,
https://doi.org/10.1007/978-3-030-66128-1_1

tion of welfare services. This is especially true for the social assistance services, which are characterised by a significant fragmentation of the actors involved and the policies produced as well as a natural dynamism (that is the direct output of evolving needs). Such fragmentation is structurally feed by the regionalisation of welfare state and social policies (Ferrera 2008), that has created the condition for relevant intra national differentiation in the definition of the models of social assistance. The extent to which this diversity can interpreted either as inequality or as an indicator of the system's capacity to differentiated the answers to social needs and/or demands in different territory (Gallego and Subirats 2012), is far beyond the scope of this book. Anyway it is a substantial topic that deserve constant attention due to the fact that pertain the dimension of social rights and the degree of the access to social provisions.

So there is a deep and intricate relationship between territorial decentralisation, local governance and government and welfare systems (Sellers and Lidström 2007). It is this context that provides the complex framework for our research effort.

The aim of the book is to provide valuable insights into the evolution of local welfare and the territorial organisation of social services by analysing the evolution of a specific organisational instrument, the *Local Area Plan*, which lies at the intersection between the themes of (sub) regional governance and models for the supply of social services. For this reason the evolution of this instrument does not pertain only to the types of policies, services and actions applied in response to social risks, but also to the organisational arrangements provided to deliver those services in a more effective and efficient way.

The focus on organisational aspects is particularly important because it is closely connected to structural and process variables like: (a) the process of change in the relationships between local actors with the enforcing, for example, of models of stabilised inter-municipal cooperation (Bouckaert et al. 2016; Turrini et al. 2010; Silva et al. 2018; Bolgherini et al. 2019); (b) the growing involvement of a plurality of actors in the governance of social services (Kazepov 2008; Bifulco and Centemeri 2008; Andreotti and Mingione 2016); and, (c) the quest for a new scale for social policies, one which involves a multilevel scale in planning and governance (Sellers and Lidström 2007; Ferrera 2008; Kazepov 2010; Kazepov and Barberis 2013).

In order to explain the organisational changes and governance shifts in local welfare, this book will attempt to reach its aim by working at the intersection of these different but interconnected aspects.

The questions this book tries to answer are few but important: what are the structural conditions that have influenced – and still do – the evolution of the Local Area Plans? What are the conditions that can lead a reform, which has as its main aim the revision of the governance structure of Local Area Plans, to be a success or a failure? Are there elements which can improve/weaken inter-municipal cooperation in an important and dynamic sector like the that of social assistance?

The research will show how these governance arrangements peculiar to Italian local welfare have changed profoundly over time, becoming both a catalyst for policies planned at different levels and a reference point for all the territorial actors involved in social policies. Furthermore, the Local Area Plans have matured their own social planning capacity over time, in a spiral that leads towards the impellent necessity to find the right equilibrium between their function as an autonomous policy planner and that of supplying policies produced at other government levels (regional and national).

While one of the ambitions for the Local Area Plan was to provide an arena in which the fragmentation of the social sector could have been recomposed, we will see that this path is far from being reached due to: (a) the complexity of the external environment; and, (b) resistance to change within the public administration sector. From this point of view, the empirical case study set out in this book, will shed light on the main drivers behind failure and success in the process of change and the evolution of Local Area Plans.

To address these questions and provide important research insights, we conducted research based on case studies focused on the Italian experience, and in particular on the Lombardy Region due to the availability of data, gathered in direct collaboration with some Local Area Plans. The methodology employed for the empirical research is a mixed one. We have used different data and different sources to reconstruct the paths to reform of our case studies. Alongside the analysis of official documents and reports, we conducted several semi-structured interviews with different actors in the network, and we had the opportunity to participate in working meetings that provided us with fresh and original qualitative data.

The book is organised as follows. In the first chapter a reconstruction of the national and regional framework will be presented, along with an analysis of the structure of ties and opportunities within which the Local Area Plans are called to act. The aim is to highlight the structural features (and limits) of the Italian and regional welfare systems in order to understand why and how Local Area Plans came about and by which context's characteristics they are influenced. In the second chapter a review of the literature dedicated to Local Area Plans will be presented, and we will attempt to give some order to the various scholarly efforts that have examined different aspects of the plans. In this chapter we will also introduce our theoretical framework; built upon a systemic approach, the framework aims at providing a possible integrated way to study the Local Area Plans experience. Of this framework we will use just one aspect to explain the object of this research, which is the propensity/resistance to organisational change/reform of Local Area Plans as the main local players in the social assistance field. The third chapter is mainly devoted to the definition of a legislative act produced by Lombardy's Government with the aim of reforming the governance structure of Local Area Plans by supporting processes of reorganisation and aggregation. Here the main implications of the law will be presented and a reflection provided on the implication of such attempts and of the reasons at the base of a substantial failure. Chapter Four is dedicated to the analysis of some cases of Local Area Plan aggregation in order to empirically study the elements that have led to the success of these attempts (or conversely, to understanding what can lead policy reform to failure). The final chapter will present the concluding remarks and some brief considerations about the future of social planning.

References

Andreotti, A., & Mingione, E. (2016). Local welfare systems in Europe and the economic crisis. *European Urban and Regional Studies, 23*(3), 252–266. https://doi.org/10.1177/0969776414557191.

Bifulco, L., & Centemeri, L. (2008). Governance and participation in local welfare: The case of the Italian Piani di Zona. *Social Policy and Administration, 42*(3), 211–227. https://doi.org/10.1111/j.1467-9515.2007.00593.x.

Bolgherini, S., Dallara, C., & Profeti, S. (2019). A shallow rationalisation? 'Merger mania' and side-effects in the reorganisation of public-service delivery. *Contemporary Italian Politics, 11*(2), 112–136. https://doi.org/10.1080/23248823.2019.1603650.

Bouckaert, G., Peters, B. G., & Verhoest, K. (2016). *Coordination of public sector organizations.* London: Palgrave Macmillan.

Ferrera, M. (2008). Dal welfare state alle welfare regions: la riconfigurazione spaziale della protezione sociale in Europa. *La rivista delle politiche sociali, 3*, 17–49.

Gallego, R., & Subirats, J. (2012). Spanish and regional welfare systems: Policy innovation and multi-level governance. *Regional & Federal Studies, 22*(3), 269–288. https://doi.org/10.1080/13597566.2012.688271.

Kazepov, Y. (2008). The subsidiarization of social policies: Actors, processes and impacts. *European Societies, 10*(2), 247–273. https://doi.org/10.1080/14616690701835337.

Kazepov, Y. (Ed.). (2010). *Rescaling social policies: Towards multilevel governance in Europe.* Ltd: Ashgate Publishing.

Kazepov, Y., & Barberis, E. (2013). *Il welfare frammentato. Le articolazioni regionali delle politiche sociali italiane.* Carocci: Roma.

Sellers, J. M., & Lidström, A. (2007). Decentralization, local government, and the welfare state. *Governance, 20*(4), 609–632. https://doi.org/10.1111/j.1468-0491.2007.00374.x.

Silva, P., Teles, F., & Ferreira, J. (2018). Intermunicipal cooperation: The quest for governance capacity? *International Review of Administrative Sciences, 84*(4), 619–638. https://doi.org/10.1177/0020852317740411.

Turrini, A., Cristofoli, D., Frosini, F., & Nasi, G. (2010). Networking literature about determinants of network effectiveness. *Public Administration, 88*(2), 528–550. https://doi.org/10.1111/j.1467-9299.2009.01791.x.

Chapter 2
The Structuration of the Italian Welfare System: From Fragmentation to Innovation

Abstract The role and the functions of the Local Area Plan are deeply influenced by the nature of the Italian welfare system. The frequent changes and adjustment in the welfare system – both at the national and local level – have intertwined with the modification of a local administrative landscape characterised by high territorial fragmentation. The need to reduce the endemic fragmentation in the welfare state provision, paved the way for the birth of the Area Local Plans. This governance arena has become the institutional place for planning and governing the social policies of the territory. The task has therefore been to consolidate the network of social services and encourage the development of a new model of local governance. At the heart of this choice is the need to strengthen the planning function in order to promote a policy model that is increasingly integrated and capable of strengthening the network of services in the territory. What have been the main (and different) legislative steps – both at the national and local level – that defines the function of Area Social Plan? what are the opportunities and the pitfalls defined by such a variegated legislative framework?

Keywords Italian welfare · Fragmentation · Local area plan · Local governance · Social assistance · Territorialisation

2.1 Introduction

The experience of the Italian Local Area Plans is part of a broader picture that pertains to the evolution of the Italian welfare system over the last 20 years. The Local Area Plans are an organisational setting aimed at resolving – among various issues –the peculiar fragmentation that exists in the supply/management of social assistance provisions at a territorial level (Bifulco and Centemeri 2008; Madama 2019; Salvati 2020).[1]

---

[1] In the next chapter we will obviously present an extensive reflection on what is and what should be the mission of the Local Area Plan, but for economy's sake in this chapter, this concise and minimal definition is sufficient to frame the issue.

© The Author(s), under exclusive license to Springer Nature Switzerland AG 2021
P. Previtali, E. Salvati, *Local Welfare and the Organization of Social Services*, https://doi.org/10.1007/978-3-030-66128-1_2

Furthermore the changes and reforms of the Italian welfare system intertwine with the modification of a local administrative landscape characterised by high territorial fragmentation through attempts to merge municipalities and reshaping competences (Fedele and Moini 2006; Previtali 2015; Bolgherini et al. 2019; Previtali and Salvati 2019). Such pervasive and constant modifications in local government and governance lead to a sort of territorial instability, characterized by a "profound, yet new, reshaping of structures, institutions, roles, competencies, borders and scale" (Teles 2016, p. 2).

This instability interlock and influence the changes in the system of local welfare, with reforms that have attempted to improve the coordination and the planning/delivery of services, through the processes of territorialisation, with the contextual aim of achieving greater customisation and more efficient interventions (Kazepov 2010; Salvati 2020).

In order to better understand the evolutionary path of Local Area Plans, a brief reconstruction of the national and regional legislative context is necessary in order to understand which ties and opportunities have influenced the definition of the Local Area Plans, and in so doing created the structural conditions for success or failure. Missed opportunities, pitfalls and reform attempts both at the national and regional level (Madama 2013) are all aspects that have heavily influenced the organisation and performances of the Italian Local Area Plans. An analytical knowledge of this landscape will provide useful tools for understanding the evolution of the Local Area Plans in the Italian welfare system, and is preparatory to the definition of an efficient theoretical framework for our analysis.

2.2   The Evolution of the Italian System of Social Assistance

The last few decades have represented a period of substantial change for welfare state systems all over Europe. These changes have been driven by new cultural paradigms such as New Public Management, which insisted on the need to rethink the role of public actors in the provision of services (Kazepov 2010), a drastic reduction in available resources due to a stricter control on budget expenditures (Andreotti and Mingione 2016), and the emergence of new and differentiated social risks (Armingeon and Bonoli 2007). All these issues, along with others, have fuelled a substantial redefinition of the welfare institutions that arose during the period of the Glorious Thirties when social protection schemes not only ensured coverage to the whole population but also played a fundamental role in stabilising European democracies (Ferrera 2020). The steady and pervasive growth of welfare systems was made possible by the process of centralising the nation state, over a long period which started in the eighteenth century and ended in the 70s (Andreotti and Mingione 2016). It was the need to ensure widespread social protection and defend the income of breadwinners (Bonoli 2005) that prompted the necessity to ensure national centralisation (Madama 2019).

The transformations that have occurred in the last 40 years due to globalisation and the post-industrial transformations of European societies (Armingeon and

Bonoli 2007), have fed the need to rethink both the scale of social provision and the role of the different institutional actors too, thus pushing towards the enforcement of regional and local welfare arrangements (Ferrera 2008; Kazepov 2010; Andreotti and Mingione 2016).

The long period of expansion of the social welfare sector has in this way also resulted in a significant transformation, over the years, in the overall institutional architecture of the European welfare state, which has led to a process of competency differentiation: while administration, management and the definition of insurance schemes for social protection should generally (for a matter of efficiency and mini-misation of costs) be centralised, the provision and planning of social services has, on the contrary, been called upon to meet local needs and peculiarities (Madama 2019).

This localisation model can be explained by the fact that it is generally consid-ered to be more efficient and better able to guarantee participatory arrangements than centralised national welfare (Bifulco and Centemeri 2008; Kazepov 2008; Andreotti and Mingione 2016).

This means that the development of social policies has been associated (particu-larly in the past decades) to an increase in the relevance of sub-national levels of government which in turn has triggered their growing demand for autonomy. These trajectories are particularly evident in regional governments who have seen a growth in their competencies and role, to the point where they have become central to many governance networks which unite public and private actors in order to define and produce policies and services that were previously under the exclusive competen-cies of national centralised governments (Ferrera 2008). In fact regions are consid-ered by theorists of multilevel governance as the third level in the structure of European polity, due to their growing institutional and budgetary autonomy and their policy competencies (Hooghe and Marks 2001).

This dynamic has stimulated a (partial) shift in the locus of powers and authority towards the lower levels of government, and by feeding the dynamics of multilevel governance has contributed to disentangling and multiplying the authority centres and, in the realm of social policies, has contributed to the territorialisation of (almost) the entire cycle of services provision, the political process at their base and to a multiplication of the actors involved (Gualini 2006; Kazepov 2010; Milio 2014; van Popering-Verkerk and van Buuren 2016). Obviously, this dynamic called for greater coordination between actors and resources, calling for joint actions of vari-ous actors involved in different and flexible arrangements, crossing sectors and lev-els of governance (Teles and Swianiewicz 2018). A condition that "impose" to the local levels of government to enforce their ability to interact and better coordinate with the other levels of government but also with their neighbours.

The various reform attempts and the search for a more optimal level in the defini-tion of social policies can also be interpreted, at least for Italy, as a possible response to the strong backwardness that still characterises social policy provisions in Southern Europe compared to the Northern and Continental countries of Europe (Bertin and Carradore 2016). The factors that contribute to the explanation of this backwardness, can be explained on one hand by the model of family and parental solidarity, which represents an adaptation to the intervention gaps of the state; here the extended family has the ability/obligation to function as a social shock absorber for its members, from caring for children and the elderly and disabled, to providing support in the event of unemployment, all of which contributes to mitigating the functional pressures for public intervention, both in the care services and in income support. On the other hand, the characteristics of the economy and of the (peripheral) labour market of Southern Europe, which is based on an underground economy as a further source of income, takes away much of the income needed to finance services from the state (Ferrera 1993; Madama 2019).

While this book has neither the ambition nor the task of offering a complete and deep reconstruction of the functioning of the Italian welfare system, for the general purpose of our research, highlighting some of its limits and critical issues will help to provide a clearer picture of the context within which the Local Area Plans are called to act.

The first characterising element of the Italian system is fragmentation and the lack of coherence and homogeneity of the intervention systems (among others Bifulco and Vitale 2006; Colombo and Regini 2016; Madama 2019). Over the years, attempts to recompose the general picture have led to no significant nor permanent results. The extensive reconfiguration of Italian welfare that has characterised the past years has continued to operate through successive stratifications, while scarce or no attention has been devoted to the rationalisation of the social measures (Madama 2019). From this point of view, Local Area Plans are a paradigmatic example: over the years they have been implicitly required to recompose the different interventions of different natures (national, regional and local) that frequently impinge on the same sector, thus feeding a fragmentation and dispersion of monetary and human resources, as well as knowledge and services.

The second element, closely connected to the first one, concerns the quest for territorial homogeneity in the provision and access to social services (Kazepov 2010). Throughout Italy, extreme heterogeneity persists, and with the exception of schemes initiated at a national level such as social allowance, household allowance and now also the Citizenship Income, we can talk more of a regional than a national welfare (Kazepov and Barberis 2013). In fact, the effective absence of real homogeneous levels of services represents an extremely delicate issue, as it increases the lack of uniformity of all those services managed at regional and/or local levels. Such situation has been amplified by the fact that institutions and legislative efforts designed to create common standards in the social rights realm have failed to intervene effectively and correct the shortages, differences and inequalities at the regional level, undermining both the system's legitimacy and its social acceptance (Colombo and Regini 2016).

The gaps are extremely wide both in terms of spending capacity, the effectiveness in services' supply and in the kind of benefits produced. This gives rise to a social citizenship which is still extremely segmented according to the place of residence, with substantial differences in the Italian municipalities' social expenditure and services provision (Gualmini and Sacchi 2016; Madama 2019). The last 20 years, have been characterised by the widening of this territorial gap, which has given rise to a multiplicity of regional and sometimes intra-regional social models which define different social rights for citizens, depending on financial availability, political preferences and the institutional capacities of the various institutional actors (Kazepov and Barberis 2013; Bertin and Carradore 2016; Colombo and Regini 2016).

As pointed out by Madama (2019), the Italian sector of social assistance and services, if compared to that of the more advanced European countries, is still, despite the reforms of the last 20 years, distinguished both by a great variety of schemes, especially categorical and local ones, and by the persistence of an under-development in the services, which results in a lack of adequate responses for certain needs, in particular for those categories that can be defined as outsiders.

In 2000, in order to recompose the extreme variability in the provision of social assistance schemes and to reduce institutional fragmentation at the local level (Kazepov and Sabatinelli 2005), the Italian government defined the first national framework for the regulation of the social assistance field, with the aim of providing – for the first time in Italian history – a national unitary scheme /plan (Madama 2013). One of the main issues National Law 328/2000 aimed to repair, was that social protection defined by regional and municipal actions and services "tended to be discretionary, uncertain in its delivery and heavily conditioned by budgetary constraints" (Madama 2013, p.4).

In the next section we will present the main aspects, both in terms of principle and policy provisions, that characterise Law No. 328, in particular with reference to the Local Area Plans.

2.3   Law No. 328/2000. An Incomplete Innovation in Social Assistance

National Law No. 328/2000 defines a framework for the creation of an integrated system of social services and interventions which has, however, remained partially unactuated in the last decade. The law's aim was to create a unitary framework for social policies, in particular through the enforcement of important elements like equal access for all citizens to social services, the effective entitlement of social rights, the strengthening of integration and a more participatory approach to policy making (Bifulco and Centemeri 2008). Law No. 328 inserted the principle of selective universalism into the system, through the creation of essential levels of social assistance (*Livelli Essenziali di assistenza sociale*, LIVEAS), with the aim of setting up common national standards for social services.

Selective universalism refers to a concept that incorporates the following points: welfare provisions and services are indifferently addressed to all citizens, but the access to them must have certain limits – connected to the economic condition of the user – as a criterion (Gualdani 2007; Gualmini and Sacchi 2016; Madama 2019). The aim of this approach is to reconcile the welfare of citizens with the fiscal and financial resource availability by making the threshold of access to services elastic and flexible and ultimately relatively modular in relation to the resources available while preserving at the same time the basic principle that welfare is intended to meet the needs of all citizens, independently from their socio-economic status.

Furthermore Law No. 328/2000, formalised a certain kind of task and authority division between states, regions and municipalities as regards competences in the social sector, hence framing a new relationship between centralised authority and local autonomies (Bifulco 2008). The law defined a set of complex arrangements able to connect a national unitary framework to a model for the local governance of social provisions based on coordination between different public actors, negotiation with territorial actors and the active participation of citizens in producing policy (Battistella et al. 2004; Bifulco and Centemeri 2008).

If we briefly consider some articles of the law, it is possible to highlight some cultural novelties inserted into it and of particular interest to our studies is the way in which the law defined the Local Area Plans as a new organisational answer to the governance of social policies.

In Article No. 1, the lawmaker defines the relevance of an integrated system of social interventions and services, aimed at guaranteeing equal quality of life and opportunities for all citizens, as well as the prevention and reduction of weaknesses connected to conditions of disability, need and discomfort due to various causes (this article aimed to give an effective answer to what is established in the Italian Constitution). The aim of this legislative provision was to state – at least theoretically – the binding need to define an equal and substantial access for all citizens to social services and provisions (the effective concretisation of social rights) throughout the national territory, despite regional differences (Gualdani 2007). In order to effectively realise this principle, the legislator considered the creation of an integrated system which reduced territorial fragmentation as fundamental. For this reason, Article No. 8 provides that the Regions, through forms of consultation with municipalities, must determine specific territorial areas (usually coinciding with the health districts already operating), essential to promoting the associated exercise of social functions. This kind of confrontation was to be preliminary to the definition of new inter-municipal forms of association responsible for delivering social services. Article No. 19 introduces the Local Area Plans as a new governance arena (Salvati 2016a), that is the inter-municipal organisational model responsible for building the integrated local system of social services and interventions. Through the Local Area Plans, the interventions that make up the overall offer of social welfare services – provided by public, private and private social actors – are defined, planned and implemented. In concrete terms, this instrument is a territorial planning document through which, in each territorial area, Municipalities and Local Health Authorities define the socio-sanitary and social policies provisions to which citizens can have access. Among the various tasks, the Law establishes that the Local Area Plans are aimed at:

(a) encouraging the formation of local systems of intervention based on complementary and flexible services and performances, which should stimulate the local resources of solidarity and self-help in particular, as well as make the citizens responsible for the planning and verification of services;
(b) qualifying expenditure by activating resources, including financial resources, derived from different forms of consultation;

(c) defining criteria for the distribution of the resources available to the Local Area Plans, and providing additional resources for the achievement of specific objectives;
(d) defining strategic objectives and priorities; and,
(e) identifying the best organisational model for the provision and integration of services.

According to this framework, the Local Area Plans must therefore contain objectives for intervention in those areas where a strong synergy between social and health services is required: minors, youth and family, the elderly, drug addiction, mental health, disability, immigration, poverty and marginalisation. This series of indications provides a picture from which the Local Area Plans can help define a truly integrated system of interventions and services, in collaboration with the various public and private territorial actors (Previtali and Salvati 2019). A situation in which the national law provides for a unitary framework able to reduce the endemic fragmentation of the Italian social assistance system and the reduction of disparities between citizens according to their regional provenience (Madama 2013), but which contextually enforces the organisational autonomy of the various territories according to their peculiarities, and stimulates social participation.

Unfortunately things for social policies have moved in another direction. A series of specific legislative choices have caused the positive coalition of factors that made possible the definition and approbation of the law to disappear (Madama 2013) and hence the provisions stated in Law No. 328 extremely difficult to implement. In particular, the 2001 Constitutional Reform and the change in the Article V of the Constitution that defines the distribution of competences between the different levels of government, have resulted in a framework which completely neglects the ambitions of Law No. 328 (Bifulco 2016; Previtali and Salvati 2019). In actual fact the Constitutional Reform enforces the Regions' powers and gives them exclusive competence in the social sector and shared competence (with the national government) in the healthcare sector, so giving them the opportunity to take on policy provisions that can be extremely different from the approach provided by Law No. 328. The Constitutional Reform had as an unintended consequence the severe undermining of the effectiveness of law by strengthening the traditional Italian fragmentation in the social policy field, an element which is exacerbated by the continuing absence of the national LIVEAS. This framework was characterised by a certain confusion and has given space to the Italian Regions to actuate completely autonomous choices in the field of social policies, so inserting into the Italian experience an additional level of fragmentation which is feeding regional particularism in the provision of social policies (Kazepov and Barberis 2013; Bifulco 2016).

From the national framework, we now turn to the analysis of the *Regione Lombardia* (Lombardy Region – RL) legislative framework which has to translate the national provisions at a regional level. The interactions between these two levels of normative action provide the structure of ties and opportunities within which Lombardy's Local Area Plans are called upon to act.

2.4   The Path Towards Law No. 3/2008: The Organisation of the Lombardy Region's Welfare Model

Law No. 3/2008 which defines the normative framework that regulates the healthcare and social services provided by RL, was drawn up in the context of the 2001 Constitutional reform which conferred broad authority and a large set of competences in the fields of social services and healthcare to the Italian regions. The approbation of Law No. 3/2008 was the first and most significant act which led to the creation of a normative and organic framework with which to rule the complex realm of Lombardy's welfare policies. Before this law, RL planned its social policies in an environment characterised by the lack of an organised and systemic model of governance and by a high level of fragmentation (as in the other Italian regions), a situation which still heavily affects the system today. Until the approbation of the law, the system was weakly regulated by Regional Law No. 1/1986 which provided for various actions in the social-assistance field, and in 1997 by a first outline of the governance model for the social-healthcare system and its territorial redefinition of the *Aziende Sanitarie Locale* (Local Healthcare Agency, ASL) and of the *Aziende Ospedaliere (Hospital Agency*, AO). This decision contributed to the striking distinction between the social and healthcare fields and to the institutionalisation of a structurally weak social dimension compared to the healthcare dimension, which persists today. Indeed over the years the hospitals and the healthcare system have increasingly become the main focus of regional government attention, both in terms of planning and resources availability, with a consequent marginalisation of the social sector.

In the aftermath of the 1997 reform, Lombardy's welfare system was structured around some ideational principles which were interpreted from a local perspective, but that were common tendencies in various European countries. The main pillar of this system was the support given to free competition among the accredited service providers, which enforces the idea of a rolling back of the public sector from service production and promotes a leading role for the market in the supply of welfare (Colombo 2012; Morel et al. 2012). The peculiar elements which characterised the regional policy making and that worked to define a coherent local welfare system were:

* the growing centrality of the accreditation system,
* the economic relevance of the social-healthcare system,
* the importance of the subsidiarity principle,
* the voucher model as the predominant model for founding the service system,
* the reorganisation of the Regional supervision and control function,
* the reorganisation of the service networks (social, social-healthcare and healthcare).

These elements were finally systematised in the Law No. 3/2008 (Previtali and Favini 2015; Previtali and Salvati 2016), the main goal of which is represented by its title *Governo della rete degli interventi e dei servizi alla persona in ambito sociale e sociosanitario* (Governance of the social and healthcare intervention networks in Local Area Plans). Under this label the main aim of the Regional government emerges and that is to regulate and structure the network of the *Unità di Offerta* (supply units, UdO) in both the social and healthcare fields. This emphasis on the organisation of the supply side instead of the demand/need side reveals the unbalanced nature of the system.

The Law first defines the following functions for the regions: policy addressing, action planning, network coordination and control regarding the compliance of the social and healthcare structures which deliver services to users. This means that the regional government embrace a regulative and control mission but avoids to steer and fully govern the system. Probably the most delicate topic is the definition of the additional standard levels for the services. These additional levels work alongside those defined by the central state; here the main problem is that while for the healthcare services the State have defined national standard levels (the so called *Livelli Essenziali di Assistenza*, essential levels of assistance, LEA), these levels have not been – and are still not – provided by the national government for the social sector. This further underlines the inferior position in which the social sector is, compared to the healthcare system.

The main ideational principle which Law No. 3/2008 revolves around, is that access to the services network is connected to the economic condition of the citizens and that they should have the freedom to choose their service supplier. The recognition of the actors' plurality is the main instrument by which the network is regulated and, *de facto*, has been defined. The recognised actors are:

- the municipalities, alone or associated in Local Area Plans, the mountain communities, ASL, and, *Aziende per i servizi alla persona* (Public Welfare Agencies, ASP);
- families, associations and informal groups;
- the Third Sector, trade unions, and profit corporations which operate in the social and/or healthcare fields and religious associations.

This law represented the first regional attempt to normatively define the network and its actors. In doing so it highlighted how the set of operators which operate in the social sector are different, and how they contribute to reaching the planning goals defined by RL. The other aim of the Law was to enforce the principle of vertical subsidiarity which reveals a kind of retreating on the part of the Region. By the means of this choice the RL keeps *per se* the planning and supervision functions within the service network, and devolves a certain freedom of action to the actors which operate at the territorial level like municipalities, the Third Sector, associations, corporations and so on.

2.5   The Structure of the RL's Local Welfare. Ideational Bases, Tasks and Instruments of the Law No. 3/2008

There are two main principles on which the Law No. 3/2008 relies, and they are the elements which have characterised the RL system in the last 20 years: (1) the reduction of the public actor's role in providing welfare services, (2) the use of organisational tools and instruments derived from the private sector, according to the theories of New Public Management (NPM).

As regards the first point, the state is considered oppressive and inefficient, unable to provide high quality services and an obstacle to promoting the potentiality of the private sector (Gori 2011). From this point of view, civil society is considered the only arena in which it is possible to produce and provide efficient social services that are able to reach all the citizens that have real needs and make a reliable use of private and public resources. The only role for the public sector is that of guaranteeing a negative freedom, in other words the removal of obstacles to the free enterprise of individuals, social groups and corporations. The concept of subsidiarity lies at the core of this model. According to this idea no organisation can control others that are weaker or are collocated at a lower level in the governance hierarchy (for example central state over local government) (Colombo 2012). In governance terms the central government should intervene only in the case of impossibility of lower institutions to effectively perform their duties. This approach rewards the autonomy of individuals and curbs state power over regional and local governments (Colombo 2012). The subsidiarity concept can be split into two elements: vertical and horizontal subsidiarity. Vertical subsidiarity concerns the level of competency of the various institutions and expects that the highest level defines standards and goals of action and supports the lowest when they are not able to guarantee their duties. Here the focus is on the type of relationship between different levels of public governance. Horizontal subsidiarity stresses the sharing of competencies, resources, functions and services between public and private/societal actors, and gives priority to the construction of networks of relationships between all the actors that operate in a given territory. Here the focus is on social interaction between different types of organisations. Vertical subsidiarity has for many years been the element that regulated the functioning of the local welfare system in the RL, where all the levels of governance involved must give priority to guaranteeing and improving the freedom of choice of the individual. This institutional vertical subsidiarity has two faces: a passive face, which means that the supra-ordered level of government (the Region) cannot fulfil tasks which are undertaken at the local level (here both public actors and private actors are considered), and should only intervene in the case of problems; and, a second active face which regards the Regional institution's efforts to create the best conditions for the local level to carry out its functions in the best possible way.

This second role is closely connected to the application of some features of the NPM's approach to the RL's social policies. Alongside the harsh criticism of the inefficiencies of the public administration, lies the idea that these inefficiencies may be overcome by the adoption of instruments used in the organisation of the private sector, and by the implementation of management criteria applied to the governance of political and social processes (Girotti 2007; Fargion 2009). This point of view is closely connected to the diffusion of the neoliberal approach to welfare state management and to public policies (Nikolai 2012); in the RL experience two elements in particular have been produced by this cultural and ideational *milieu*. The first is the empowerment of citizens through the implementation of mechanisms which enforce their freedom of choice, and perceives them more as consumers than citizens. The second is the need to shape the welfare system around the principle of competition between providers which are – at least partially – funded by public resources. In this way, the citizen/user is free to choose the supplier which best responds, in their opinion, to their needs.

Besides these two goals, it is possible to define one main task/principle from which all the others derive: the promotion of citizen's freedom of choice within the services network. From the various interviews conducted and documents consulted stems the fact that this one principle has been considered by the regional government fundamental to respecting the dignity of all individuals, but it is also been identified as the instrument through which a open access to the service network has been pursued. The law constituted the normative ground for enforcing this freedom by providing instruments to create a kind of "quasi-market" of social and healthcare services (Salamon 2012). In this quasi-market the public actor keeps *per se* the supervision of the sector's functioning while at the same time devolving the production of services to other independent organisations (private and/or public actors), which compete to gain clients. They are funded by the users or, more frequently, by public (or semi-public) agencies which buy the services and act as an agent on behalf of the users (Le Grand 2007, 2011).

In this scenario the user choses not only from which supplier to buy the service but also which type of service he prefers; this opens up, at least theoretically, an opportunity for the user and his family to personalise their pattern of care and define the quality of their life within the services network. These features go along with the guarantee provided by the Region regarding the entitlement to open access to the network and the assurance of the system taking responsibility. By means of these legislative choices, the Region steps back from the function of unique services producer and tailors for itself the role of the system guarantor, entitled to supervising the functioning of the net and to defining the actors allowed to provide services in it, while the citizen/user becomes perfectly (at least theoretically) autonomous and fully responsible for their choices.

The instrument which enables the users' free choice is, as previously said, the quasi-market of services. This market is composed of the public sector and the private profit and non-profit actors, with prominence being given to the latter two due to the principle that the public sector should only regulate and supervise the network. For this reason the law explicitly outlines the main responsibilities of the Region as being the functions of planning, buying and supervision. These functions are accomplished through its territorial structures, the *Azienda Sanitaria Locale*.

The goal of the regional legislator is to make the quasi-market the real driving force of the system, and to effectively realise this goal it has created a complex structure of incentives (vouchers, money transfer, bonus etc.) which give the users the opportunity to freely chose the service provider. The Region has the duty of guaranteeing the rules are respected and of providing a quality standard, in particular through an accreditation system: through this choice it is possible to connect the incentives to the improvement of a system based on competition between the different suppliers.

The voucher model is the main instrument through which the quasi-market works. Thanks to this model of service purchase, the Region ensures the user's freedom of choice and supports market competition: the goal is to enforce the relationship between efficiency, effectiveness, free choice and competition among providers. According to Regional government, this provision should improve the efficiency of the system by forcing the providers in a competitive regime to increase their attention towards and proximity to users, hence positively influencing the quality of the services. Simultaneously, an increase in efficiency would be the product of a better use of the resources: this is the idea that the private sector can do better with the same (or even less) resources. From this approach stems the idea that the economic parameter becomes essential for evaluating the performances of the system, even more so after the explosion of the crisis in 2008 and the reduction of available resources (Hemerijck 2012; Morel et al. 2012).

The supply side is at the centre of the Law No. 3/2008, rather than the demand side or the analysis of the social needs. The task of improving the freedom of choice and the desire to promote market competition, inevitably sheds light on the providers, who are the central actors of a system in which citizens/users have a direct relationship with them.

From this point of view the support given to the actors of the Third Sector (TS) is particularly relevant, the aim of which is to enforce their role within the network as a service producer and provider, and to recognise their role during the policy planning phase. This function was formalised by the TS's participation in the permanent consultation forum opened up in the RL and in particular by involving the TS in territorial planning through the Local Area Plans. The Local Area Plans have in this way become, over the years, the institutional arena in which the non-profit sector can deliver its contribution both to the planning and the implementation phases (Salvati 2016a).

The Regional government's focus on the role of the TS is due to the high level of flexibility that characterises its actions, and its ability to mobilise social resources which would otherwise be fragmented and unused (Franzoni and Anconelli 2014). This choice has led to the valorisation of the social capital of the region, by promoting the role and the organisation of the civil society (Kreuter and Lezin 2002), and by trying to reduce the risk that the citizen/user could be quashed within the mechanism of the impersonal bureaucratic system. A system founded on the prominent role of bureaucracy is a system based on a strong asymmetry of resources and information, a limit which may result decisive in the production of social-healthcare services and in particular for the users' access to this network (Bouckaert et al. 2016).

2.6   Territorialisation. Conceptualising the Governance of Local Welfare

In the aftermath of the 2008 crisis, the need to keep expenditure on social policies under control while at the same time guaranteeing a high performing welfare system, able to trigger major social – economic integration and control the ever increasing risk of social exclusion, made it indispensable for European governments to continue redefining their welfare state provisions. A valuable framework for interpreting part of the modifications that occurred may be the intersection of two structurally changing paths: a new organisation of welfare governance (Kazepov 2010; Andreotti and Mingione 2016) and the production of policies more oriented to the mobilisation and activation of social resources than to simple protection (Bifulco 2008). This has led to the delineation of a long term phase of territorialisation of welfare as the instrument to enforce activation processes. With activation we are referring to that policy process whose main aim is to ensure social inclusion through policies focused on labour, social assistance, and the fight against poverty and which relies on the principle of the empowerment of the individual and the community (Geldof 1999; Bifulco 2008).

The first element which influences this change – as stated at the beginning of the chapter – is the process of reorganising the public authority by decentralising powers and competencies to the local dimension, as the administrative level which fosters policies. The governance model becomes a crucial element to understanding the (eventual) changes in the production of social policies (Previtali and Salvati 2019). A fundamental element of the governance's realm is the coordination and integration of actors and organisations and, as a derived consequence, the cooperation pathways among actors – frequently collected on a multilevel scale (Ferrera 2008; Kazepov 2010; Teles 2016) – and the emergence of the arenas of governance (Bifulco 2005; Trigilia 2005; Salvati 2016a, 2020) as institutionalised spaces in which various actors (public, profit, non-profit, associations etc.) are called upon to influence and define parts of social policies.

If we apply this framework to planning and production in local welfare, four elements take on an essential role (Bifulco 2016; Salvati 2020): (a) the role performed by local administrations and governance networks in decision-making processes; (b) the organisational arrangements defined to plan, produce and supply services, (c) the interdependence of factors conditioning well-being, such as housing, work, access to health services etc.; and, (d) the idea that at the local scale integrated interventions in harmony with the needs/requests of a community are to be favoured.

The new challenges to welfare systems, both at national and local level, oblige the involved actors – both in the public and the private sector – to rethink and modernise the welfare model and its characteristics, both in terms of services produced and in terms of social protection models, while maintaining as their target the answers to new social needs which are emerging at the local level with the specific configurations of local context (Andreotti et al. 2012).

All the institutions of the local governance are called upon to act in a more coordinated way, thus implementing networks of horizontal governance instead of vertical governance (Klijn and Koppenjan 2000). These networks, as the Lombardy case highlights (Bifulco 2008; Salvati 2016), should be characterised by a high level of cooperation and dynamism, which involves both the public institutions acting at the territorial level and the private actors, and the implementation of an institutionalised network for cooperation (Klok et al. 2018; Salvati 2020). Under these provisions, as happened in Italy and as exemplified by the evolution of the Lombardy case, these relationships are increasingly putting the municipalities at their centre, hence making them the fulcrum of a rooted institutional network which is responsible for social policies (Fedele and Moini 2006; Lecy et al. 2014; Salvati 2016b). This means that the network models applied at local level to institutionalise inter-municipal cooperation and boost coordination assume a fundamental role (Bel and Warner 2015; Teles 2016).

This process has recently been enforced in Italy by the strengthening of the Regions' powers in some fields like energy, tourism, healthcare and social policies, with the last two competencies triggering the need to rethink the social protection model and push forward towards a greater proximity between institutions (planning phase), providers (supply phase) and citizens. The proximity between services, the Local Area Plans and users and the ambition to provide efficient answers to social needs (Andreotti and Mingione 2016), are the ideational and political pillars at the base of this pattern of change, which has imposed a new process of territorialisation, and fostered a radical change in social policy production and governance (Centemeri et al. 2006; Kazepov and Barberis 2013; Salvati 2016a).

While, according to Bifulco (2016), territorialisation can produce uncertainty in the policy making and implementation process – but this, according to literature, heavily depends on the different arrangements of local governance (among others Folta 1998; Previtali and Salvati 2019) -, it also has the undeniable advantage of enforcing the participation process of citizens and associations, strengthening the involvement of private actors and triggering greater transparency and inclusiveness.

The second element which influences this change is the redefinition of the principles and main goals of welfare, with the aim of moving the system from a logic of curing and repairing to a logic of preparing and activating. The new knowledge based economy of the globalised world, the limits in the spending capacity of states and the emergence of new social risks and needs (single parenthood, need to reconcile work time and private life, precarious contracts etc.) all call for new dynamic forms of social protection (Bonoli 2005).

A new model based on policies that invest in human capital development, in childcare, in education, in support and the requalification of the unemployed, and in a new safeguarding and empowerment of families: all these are the factors that qualify social policies as a strategic investment, and define a new policy logic called "social investment" (Esping-Andersen et al. 2002; Jenson and Saint-Martin 2003; Morel et al. 2012).

The basis of this concept is an idea which emerges partially as a critique against the neoliberal approach, which has dominated from the beginning of the eighties and in which welfare state expenditures are considered a weight that is an obstacle to economic growth and a leverage which gives too much space for the direct intervention of the state. The main idea of the social investment approach is that we are facing a time of great changes in the economic and social order, and that we need more effective and flexible instruments to fight social exclusion (Morel et al. 2012) the main enemy against which the welfare state is committed. The new inspiring principle is that social policies should help prevent people falling into social/economic exclusion and minimise the inter-generational transfer of poverty. A challenge that obviously directly involves the government levels closer to citizens.

This approach sees the promotion of individuals' capabilities as a strategic investment, and shares the neoliberal paradigm idea that resources should be employed to activate individuals and families through positive incentives like (re) collocating them in the labour market or supporting them through social-health weaknesses, not through passive benefits or simple money transfer (Morel et al. 2012).

From this perspective the state and the public actors turn out to have a new positive role, because they have the opportunity to repair market failures which negatively affect economic and social outcomes. The state provides the framework and the tools to improve human capital and guarantee safeguards against social risks and in coordination with private actors, associations, the Third Sector etc., can build a net in which efficiency, economic growth and social inclusion are reconciled (Morel et al. 2012).

This kind of cooperation, which is different from the neoliberal laissez faire focused on the production and supply of services, creates a fertile ground from which the growth of some cooperative and innovative experiences like community welfare can emerge (Powell and Barrientos 2004).

Community welfare is a peculiar form of welfare mix and the logic behind it is not merely based on the assumption of the pluralisation of actors involved in the delivery of services, but rather is more focused on the pluralisation of the functioning rules and in their logic of actions (Ponzo 2014). This means that within a certain model of community welfare – that is territorially defined – we can find various regulative models and causes of actions that can produce different policymaking experimentations.

According to Ponzo, there are four logics of actions involved in community welfare: state, market, communitarian/associative and family. This means that actors can operate according to different logics within the same network, thus enriching and multiplying the opportunities of actions for the community. From these nested logics we can assume that four main actors are involved: public institutions, market, families and community (community is composed of actors like associations, non-profits, churches etc.). So, the elements which define community welfare are (Ponzo 2014):

- the equal role exerted by different actors. The State is not supra ordered compared to the private actors, but operates to coordinate the various societal efforts and promote an "enabling state";
- citizens (and their families) are not only users but also welfare producers. In this logic they are not simply customers that choose between different services and providers but are stakeholders in the system;
- the main targets of the actions are not only the users but the whole community, and the aim is to improve everyone's wellbeing.

These elements are extremely important also because they define a policy dynamic that positively influenced and enforced the process of welfare territorialisation.

The territorialisation concept with regards to policy making, concerns the tendency to adopt an integrated approach to a complex set of problems (social, healthcare, economic, etc.) related to the specific needs of a delimited area, and takes the territory as its reference point for policies and interventions (Bifulco 2016; Salvati 2016a). This principle, applied to social policy, affirms that welfare provisions should be constructed at the lowest possible level, as this enables the most practical provision of effective social protection tailored to individual needs (as far as it is possible) (Martelli 2006; Ranci 2006).

The economic crisis has had variable negative effects both in terms of the transformation of the demand for social protection and in terms of the supply of welfare supports (Hemerijck 2012). Furthermore, in this context, we can say that maybe too much hope has been placed on territorialisation as a means of generating innovations for citizens (Andreotti and Mingione 2016). Likewise, the results of partnership arrangements, central-to-local responsibility devolutions – or participatory processes – have produced mixed results in different countries.

In the RL the enforcing of the territorialisation process intertwines with the necessity to enforce integration between the healthcare and the social dimensions, an issue that has been a constant thorn in the RL's side over the last decades (Carabelli and Facchini 2011; Fosti et al. 2012). This is because this kind of integration should be built up properly from the lowest level of the policy process governance, as it is this level that is in direct contact with citizens' needs and operators' competencies/actions. This integration is probably the main strategic goal pursued by the Regional government in the aftermath of the 3/2008 law, in order to overcome the structural fragmentation of services and actions that have characterised regional policy making over the past 20 years. Among the various attempts it is possible to quote, for example, the definition of the so-called integrated access to services, a path (theoretically) able to follow the user along all the services' chain. In particular this goal would be reached by strengthening the *Punto unico di accesso* (Unified access point, PUA), whose duty it is to take responsibility for the citizen and support them on their path within the network. These territorially based access points, which have to collect data on users, have resulted fairly ineffective because they proved insufficient for recomposing the fragmentation of information, knowledge and actions that affected the system due to the lack of integration between the territorial services, the limits of the web infrastructure and the lack of personnel.

Despite this difficulty in effectively reaching a high level of integration, the path towards a stronger territorialisation carried on and its actually under this "label" that we can place the legislative effort made by the RL to institutionalise at a regional level the existence of the Local Area Plans through the Law No. 3/2008 and the 3 year recurring *Linee guida per la pianificazione zonale* (guidelines for Local Area Plan planning activity) (Previtali and Favini 2016).

As we have seen, the creation of Local Area Plans has probably been the main central state organisational/governance answer to the extreme fragmentation that characterises the Italian model of social services planning and supply (Battistella et al. 2004; Bifulco and Centemeri 2008; Bifulco 2016; Salvati 2016a). This structural fragmentation has had a permanent negative influence over the social service system that has led to weak coordination between the various institutional levels involving different public responsibility, mainly regional and municipal, and has produced huge differences between territories and disparity of rights (Bifulco 2016; Martelli 2006). From here, the perspective of integration set out by Law No. 328/2000, which defines a framework for the creation of an integrated system of social services and interventions closely linked to a model of local governance based on negotiation and participation. Under Art. No. 19 of the law, Italian municipalities have to unite in new inter-municipal groupings called Local Area Plans, which are the instruments for the associated planning of services and social interventions of municipalities able to match the resources, and respond to the needs, falling within a limited territorial area (Battistella et al. 2004).

According to law, the Local Area Plans should fulfil tasks concerning social services which require a strong synergy between health and social services: minors, families, elderly, addictions, mental health, disability, immigration, poverty and social exclusion. That is why the Local Area Plans are a strategic institutional tool for achieving integration between the two sectors. The Local Area Plans act according to the main principles defined by the Lombardy Region, that are: the centrality of the individual, the support to families as the fundamental nucleus for a person's care, flexible services, and the possibility for citizens to choose freely among the various structures of the regional social – health network.

2.7   The Impact of the Regional Law No. 23/2015 on the RL's Welfare: Ideational and Organisational Changes

Law No. 23/2015 is the most important legislative action taken by the Regional government since the approbation of the Law No. 3/2008, and can be considered a significant turning point for regional local welfare, because it affects two constitutive elements of the system: the ideational dimension/the principles – from which policy goals derive – and the organisational model – which defines how the system works and how it accomplishes its duties.

Despite the fact that the political majority which leads the Region is always a centre right majority, the change of presidency has led to a partial change in their approach towards local welfare. More communitarian elements have been inserted into the neoliberal model, which enforce the governance role of the Regional government, support the strengthening of community welfare and provide a different approach towards the subsidiarity model. Law No. 23 has the goal of creating a systemic framework by which to systematise the RL's normative production, which over the years has oscillated from the overregulation of the social sector (in the eighties till the first half of the nineties) to the reorganisation of healthcare management and the partial marginalisation of the social sector.

The first assumption from which the new legislator started in projecting the reform was the need to rethink the organisational model which was too focused on the role of the hospital and explicitly healthcare centred: according to the new regional government, this approach was not able to cope with the new challenges. The main ideational principle was the shift from "cure" to "take care of", which means that the system should not be simply focused on curing health or social-health weaknesses, but has the duty to overcome the fragmentation of measures and actions, and move towards a more complex taking charge of the multiple fragilities which affect vulnerable people. The new paradigm is that social and economic exclusion, social vulnerability, the cure of illnesses, the support of single users and families affected by economic difficulties or unemployment, are different aspects of a single problem.

The new reform had the goal of creating an integrated, tailored and appropriate social-healthcare assistance plan, which could cope with the expression of new social-health fragilities, and which shifted the focus from the providing phase to the prevention phase, in order to manage social and health disadvantages. According to the various actors involved in the actuation of the reform, the main issue is to avoid that a single need could become chronic and trigger the emergence of other different needs.

In order to fulfil these tasks some systemic actions which revolve around two critical points have been deployed: a global and multidimensional responsibilisation of the user (a theme that is now recurring in the Local Area Plans' planning documents) and the strengthening of a welfare system based on two pillars; a) the supply provided by the accredited UdO and b) the group of integrated measures/actions governed by the voucher system, which are funded by the Family Fund instituted with the Regional Decree No. 116/2013.

This Decree opened up to new legislature which aimed at providing support to the role of the family and its actions; support to the family with fragile components and complex pathologies, support for non-autonomous people, and support for users with chronic-degenerative pathologies who live in poverty, all the while safeguarding the principle of subsidiarity but also enforcing the ties with the other actors that operate within the social service network. In this way the family is recognised as being a main actor in the welfare system not just as a passive receiver or service user but also as a welfare producer, from a perspective that is in line with that of the welfare mix (Jung 2010).[2]

The attention placed on support for innovative experimentation and the measures of the second pillar of welfare, have as their main goal the opening up of the system to a new model able to provide appropriate and flexible answers to social needs which were not being taken care of in the traditional services network. The main problem is how to improve access to the network and make it more flexible so as to provide a set of differentiated answers.

Concerning the social services network, Law No. 23 stresses the centrality of the so called *Valutazione Multidimensionale del Bisogno* (multidimensional needs assessment, VMD), which defined the rules of the social-healthcare system for the

---

[2] An approach that will be explicitly stated in a Regional legislative act like the Regional Decree No. 7631/2017 concerning the new Local Area Plans guidelines for the 2018–2020 period.

year 2014. This led to a scale that aims to evaluate all the needs of an individual and/ or a family, by taking into consideration various aspects (social, economic, familial, healthcare), and that allows an integrated reading of multiple needs to be provided, easier access to the services net and the provision of overall support within it (The VMD is the element which had the Local Area ambition to fix a structural deficit of the system, that is the extreme fragmentation of the actions, resources and knowledge that characterise the RL's welfare system).

The VMD – for which the ASL (now the ATS) and the municipalities are responsible – may be considered as the tool which concretely promotes the improvement of integration in the territory, by applying what is stated by Law No. 23 that a close relationship between the social and the healthcare systems is essential to promoting the continuity of assistance for citizens. The interviews we carried out with Regional officials and the Region's counsellors revealed that what is fundamental for the evolution of the system is for the two sectors to perform more integrated work, an integration that should be pursued at the territorial level. Furthermore they stated that the Regional government considers a successful integration to include renewed attention to social-economic vulnerability, which reinforces social inclusion and integration even if clear parameters and indicators for the measuring of this policy task have not been defined.

2.8 The New Organisational Model. Welfare Territorialisation and Regional Decrees for Social Planning

The first element to consider as a possible explanation for a changing pattern, is the effort to improve the connection between territory and services. The new presidency moved quickly forward in this direction with the new Law No. 23/2015 which totally rebuilt the local structure of governance. The old ASL and AO were substituted by two new organisations which were separated according to their functions: the *Azienda socio sanitaria Territoriale* (Territorial Social Healthcare public body, ASST) is the provider of all the services produced by the Region in the social healthcare and healthcare sectors, while the *Agenzia per la Tutela della salute* (Health Protection Agency, ATS) has a governance function: it supervises the functioning of the healthcare and social services networks and supports the integration between the two. The reform, without a clear legislative provision dedicated to the social dimension, implicitly stated that the responsibility and the governance of the social services is completely in the hands of municipalities and Local Area Plans, and that they should be supported by the ATS in this function (even if it is not clear how and with which mission, except for the strengthening of the integration between the social and healthcare dimensions).

In order to realise the integration between the social and healthcare dimensions in the territory, the reform perceives the ATS as the structure responsible for the governance of this process. For this reason the *Dipartimento per la Programmazione per l'integrazione delle Prestazioni Sociosanitarie e Sociali* (Planning department for the integration of healthcare and social services, PIPSS) was created. The goal of this department is to develop the new strategic functions of analysis and governance of the social and healthcare needs, and is the place where the governance of the taking responsibility for the individual and the families in the social and healthcare networks are planned. The main functions of the department are to effectively pursue the integration between the two networks, improve innovative actions on the territory and strengthen the integrated taking responsibility for the users. Furthermore the department has the duty of technically supporting another organisational model that is part of the ATS, the so called *Cabina di Regia* (control room, CdR) which is the arena where mayors, ATS, ASST and the actors of the territory plan the policies to realise, share common experiences, problems and best practices and try to improve the integration both between the networks, and between the different institutional and private actors working in the territory. The ATS, according to the new legislative provision, becomes a true arena of governance, the only network in which all the local actors involved in social and healthcare service provision can effectively share stances, interests and problems. Moreover it represents the institutionalisation of the social policies territorialisation process at the local level.

An evident shortcoming of the reform is the fact that a general framework for the planning and delivery of social services was not provided. It has *de facto* reduced the role of the Law No. 3/2008, leaving it modified and weakened without defining a new framework for social policies. From this point of view the only possible action would have been the definition of a law dedicated exclusively to the definition of an integrated system of social offer. The absence of a framework law for the definition of a "social supply network", left all the organisation of the sector to (a) the Local Area Plans and municipalities, (b) the different, fragmented and sometimes contradictory, legislative actions provided by the regional government, and (c) to the "good will" of the ATS to territorially promote a process of integration between the social and the healthcare dimensions.

In any case, this is simply the last step of a process that has seen over the past years a growing centrality assigned to Local Area Plans, both for national choices and Regional Government decisions (the different regional decrees for Local Area Plan's social planning and the different regional policies for the socio-assistance field). Despite this evolution, the increasing importance of the Local Area Plan has not been side-lined by a growth in the available resources or by a widespread consciousness among municipalities about the strategic importance of organisationally enforcing Local Area Plans.

If we take the year 2008 as a reference point with the approbation of the new regional Law No. 3/2008 on social-healthcare services, we can briefly look at the evolution of the Lombardy experience. The planning of the Local Area Plans for the 3-year period 2009–2011 was part of a new regulatory context, defined by the regional Law No. 3/2008. For this reason the principles on which it was built are those that have characterised the evolution of the RL's welfare as stated by the Law No. 3/2008: the centrality of the person and support to the family, as a fundamental nucleus for personal care, the flexibility of services and the citizens right to choose their preferred structure for the supply of services.

The 2012–2014 guidelines theoretically opened a new phase in the planning of social services and in the definition of the Local Area Plans role, in particular because they:

- focused on the institutional and financial re-composition of interventions, decisions and programming guidelines;
- provided a simplification in the administrative fulfilments required of Local Area Plans;
- aimed to carry out local experimentations of a promotional welfare (the welfare mix model).

The Local Area Plans central and strategic role in the network was substantially emphasised by the Regional guidelines for the social planning of the triennium 2015–2017. The main goal was to build up a new planning model centred on a territory's needs; a step considered preparatory to obtaining a more effective analyses of social needs and fundamental to defining more innovative and performative actions. The focus was on the enforcing of the local welfare services network. Through this new approach, the Local Area Plans became the strategic territorial actors in the local governance, because they were the only instruments able to define a planning effort effectively rooted on the territory and its social needs (Salvati 2016a). By means of this choice local welfare and its actors have now the duty of reading the manifold needs present in our society in an integrated way, with the goal of responding to the needs with the most effective and appropriate policy.

These actions were fairly inevitable, and were moved by the need to rethink and modernise the interventions included in the welfare system, both in terms of services provided and in terms of protection models linked to new needs (Ferrera 1998; Salvati 2016b). New needs are increasingly pressing in a morphologically and socially articulated territory like the RL.

These processes of change are naturally influenced by the specific territorial contexts in which social protection networks have arisen and developed; the change in welfare occurs because an imbalance is created between practical solutions and new problems, to solve which old policies are no longer sufficient and for this reason the solutions change in order to adapt to new problems and new needs (Ferrera 1993).

This DGR gave Local Area Plans the opportunity to rethink their role and contribute to the reduction of the fragmentation but, practically, the regional government did not provide the Local Area Plans with instruments and tools to effectively combat such fragmentation. As far as services and resources are concerned, a relevant fragmentation persists due to the numerous policies produced at a national and regional level that the Local Area Plans have to implement and the difficulty in reducing the different streams of financing. A better attempt has been made in the sharing of knowledge through the introduction of new technological instruments to integrate and provide new datasets able to gather different data and sources of data. The so called *Cartella Sociale Informatizzata* (CSI) is an essential tool for the social services of municipalities and Local Area Plans, as it enables the management of users' social information, connection to other databases and the fulfilment of national and regional information transfer requirements.

As emerged from our interviews, it is the territorialisation of welfare and the strengthening of the local level that are, according to the Regional government, the best instruments for enforcing the process of policy production and its implementation. It improves the participatory and transparency level (Bifulco 2008; Bifulco and Centemeri 2008), and imposes a continuous improvement model in the service provision that is the only way to promote a better analysis of new and complex needs; the focus, as stated in the interviews with the networks' stakeholders, is to improve social inclusion by individuating the fight against new forms of poverty, the improvement of new processes of social activation and the definition of a new model of cooperation between actors, with a more proactive role being taken by the Region and the local institutions.

Both the functionaries of the Region and the representatives of the Local Area Plans, confirmed that with the new organisational model produced by the Law No. 23/2015, the functions of the Local Area Plans have opened up a new path, which move Local Area Plans from the simple function of management/(partial)supplier to that of an actor able to: read and analyse social needs in the territory, plan actions to fight these needs, promote innovation in social policies, and coordinate the various actors of the network.

In order to promote these changes, the RL's legislative approach has partially changed, because new actions and measures in the social fields should – at least theoretically – fulfil four requisites:

- *promptness*: providing quick answers to needs (if possible, enhancing the prevention phase);
- *temporariness*: the actions must have a defined time and course of action, connected to the particular needs and related to the individual project as defined by the social assistance (avoiding "welfarism" and the simple transfer of money, and avoiding dependence on social services);
- *joint–responsibilities*: getting out of a condition of poverty and need is achieved through a common effort between institutions, operators and citizens;
- *tailored*: the single projects should be fostered according to the single user's need (using the deployed policy tools), in order to improve their autonomy.

The task of policy production is no longer exclusively focused on the enforcing of the market and on the strong emphasis on freedom of choice and horizontal subsidiarity, but is related also to the (attempt at) construction – cooperatively carried out by the RL and the various actors on the territory – of a broader welfare network, able to support those in a weak socio-economic condition and to enforce the level of social inclusion by fighting against vulnerability.

The aim of this choice is to change the core of the system because in the previous years the focus was on the predominance of the supply side, the support to the providers and to the structures, with the result that a fairly rigid system was drowned with depersonalised actions. Now the system is focused on new needs, and on constructing a social services network as flexible and as personalised as possible. The individualisation of policies concerns: the individualisation of entitlement, tailor made interventions, and the promotion and support of a citizen's ability to create an independent life project (Valkenburg 2007). These kinds of actions, due to their high level of personalisation, can be effective only if they are thought out and realised in proximity to the citizens, and that is why the implementation of these new welfare provisions needs a strong degree of decentralisation to be effective (Bifulco 2008). In order to enforce this kind of action what is apparently missing is the commitment towards the definition of an organic and coherent "system of social supply", a system composed not only of residential and semi residential structures, but that embraces a coherent system of social policies and measures, based on an effective reduction in the fragmentation of dispersed resources and data knowledge. A system effectively aimed at constructing an instrument of broad coordination between the different actors involved in the socio-assistance field.

In order to actually improve this new network, the directors of the ATS and the ASST addressed their attention to some critical points to tackle in order to have a more effective system of services provision. The first issue concerned the need to simplify the bureaucratic steps and make it easier for citizens to access and remain within the network; a possible solution could be the effective implementation of a welfare front office able to support citizens on their journey within the network. The second relevant element is the need to improve and better institutionalise the working relationship between the ATS, the ASST and Local Area Plans: these three actors have the responsibility of integrating and reducing fragmentation, but to do this, they need time and organisational instruments. Enforcing the *Cabina di Regia* has been identified as the best way to reach this goal, to further improve the territorialisation of the policy making planning phase.

Similar considerations were made by the Local Area Plan representatives, who underlined the need to provide a more effective and integrated services supply chain as an instrument for managing new emerging needs. This kind of chain is necessary to guarantee a better continuity in the taking responsibility for the users and could represent a step forward in reducing the level of fragmentation in the system. Moreover it is necessary to enforce the coordination ties among actors also in order to provide policy answers that in this historical moment need to be more multi sectoral because they contextually involve different areas of actions (i.e. housing, poverty, unemployment, disability etc.) and different actors.

Providing a clear definition of the boundaries of the social services network is considered by the ATS, the ASST, Local Area Plans, the Third Sector and for-profit private actors as a central topic. Who are the subjects that make up the network? And more importantly: how is it possible to integrate all these subjects into the system's governance? An interview with the TS representatives shed light on this problem, which is closely connected to that of the accreditation system: in order to have a more effective and integrated system it is also necessary to improve the quality of the services provided. Their words echo the statement made by the directors of the ATS and ASST who claimed that in order to have an effective services chain able to intercept new needs and new poverties, the chain should be characterised by a high level of flexibility and individualisation of the actions.

As outlined in the reconstruction of the complex path covered in the last few years in Lombardy, Local Area Plans have become the institutional places for planning and governing the social policies of the territory. An evolution for this arena that has moved along with the changes occurring to the entire system of regional welfare. The task has therefore been to consolidate the network of social services and encourage the development of a new model of local governance. At the heart of this choice is the need to strengthen the planning function in order to promote a policy model that is increasingly integrated and capable of strengthening the network of services in the territory. The strengthening of the Local Area Plans, as it has been set out over the last decade, is the primary requirement for overcoming the "single" approach, so that the different actors involved in the planning can on the one hand recognise their own peculiarities, i.e. their resources and critical points, and on the other hand recognise the local reality as the seat of the new planning and as a place within which to build connections and relationships between the different actors.

Both the reconstruction of the national and regional framework highlighted some worrisome problems: (a) the need to curb fragmentation through the definition of governance arrangements that, like Local Area Plans, can stimulate and support inter-municipal cooperation, (b) the impellent necessity to boost institutional and multi actor coordination as a possible resolution of the fragmentation issue, especially in a sector like the one of social assistance characterised by a multiplicity of actors and schemes of intervention, and (c) trying to solve the governance of the governance issue (Previtali and Salvati 2019) by identifying innovative organisational models and implementing reforms able to solve collective action problems, agency loss, policy learning etc.

It is from this perspective that the various reform attempts can be interpreted, as well as the last Local Area Plans planning regional decree for the years 2018–2020 that represents a significant and straightforward turning point in social planning and an effort at organisational reorientation, as we will see in the next chapters.

References

Andreotti, A., & Mingione, E. (2016). Local welfare systems in Europe and the economic crisis. *European Urban and Regional Studies, 23*(3), 252–266. https://doi.org/10.1177/0969776414557191.

Andreotti, A., Mingione, E., & Polizzi, E. (2012). Local welfare systems: A challenge for social cohesion. *Urban Studies, 49*(9), 1925–1940. https://doi.org/10.1177/0042098012444884.

Armingeon, K., & Bonoli, G. (Eds.). (2007). *The politics of post-industrial welfare states: Adapting post-war social policies to new social risks*. London: Routledge.

Battistella, A., De Ambrogio, U., & Ranci Ortigosa, E. U. D. (2004). *Il piano di zona: costruzione, gestione, valutazione*. Roma: Carrocci Editore.

Bel, G., & Warner, M. E. (2015). Inter-municipal cooperation and costs: Expectations and evidence. *Public Administration, 93*(1), 52–67. https://doi.org/10.1111/padm.12104.

Bertin, G., & Carradore, M. (2016). Differentiation of welfare regimes: The case of Italy. *International Journal of Social Welfare, 25*(2), 149–160. https://doi.org/10.1111/ijsw.12183.

Bifulco, L. (2005). *Le politiche sociali*. Roma: Carocci.

Bifulco, L. (2008). Politiche pubbliche e partecipazione. Alcune piste per la comparazione fra Italia e Franca. *Rivista italiana di politiche pubbliche, 3*(2), 65–91. https://doi.org/10.1483/27437.

Bifulco, L. (2016). Citizenship and governance at a time of territorialization: The Italian local welfare between innovation and fragmentation. *European Urban and Regional Studies, 23*(4), 628–644. https://doi.org/10.1177/0969776414531969.

Bifulco, L., & Centemeri, L. (2008). Governance and participation in local welfare: The case of the Italian Piani di Zona. *Social Policy and Administration, 42*(3), 211–227. https://doi.org/10.1111/j.1467-9515.2007.00593.x.

Bifulco, L., & Vitale, T. (2006). Contracting for welfare services in Italy. *Journal of Social Policy, 35*(3), 495–513. https://doi.org/10.1017/S0047279406009895.

Bolgherini, S., Dallara, C., & Profeti, S. (2019). A shallow rationalisation? 'Merger mania' and side-effects in the reorganisation of public-service delivery. *Contemporary Italian Politics, 11*(2), 112–136. https://doi.org/10.1080/23248823.2019.1603650.

Bonoli, G. (2005). The politics of the new social policies: Providing coverage against new social risks in mature welfare states. *Policy & Politics, 33*(3), 431–449. https://doi.org/10.1332/0305573054325765.

Bouckaert, G., Peters, B. G., & Verhoest, K. (2016). *Coordination of public sector organizations*. London: Palgrave Macmillan.

Carabelli, G., & Facchini, C. (Eds.). (2011). *Il modello lombardo di welfare: continuità, riassestamenti, prospettive*. Milano: Franco Angeli.

Centemeri, L., de Leonardis, O., & Monteleone, R. (2006). Amministrazioni pubbliche e Terzo Settore nel welfare locale. La territorializzazione delle politiche sociali tra delega e congestione. *Studi organizzativi, 1*, 145–170.

Colombo, A. (2012). Principle of subsidiarity and Lombardy: Theoretical background and empirical implementation. In A. Colombo (Ed.), *Subsidiarity Governance. Theoretical and empirical models* (pp. 3–17). New York: Palgrave.

Colombo, S., & Regini, M. (2016). Territorial differences in the Italian 'social model'. *Regional Studies, 50*(1), 20–34. https://doi.org/10.1080/00343404.2013.879641.

Esping-Andersen, G., Gallie, D., Hemerijck, A., & Myles, J. (2002). Why we need a new welfare state. Oxford University Press, USA.

Fargion, S. (2009). *Il servizio sociale. Storia, temi e dibattiti*. Roma-Bari: Laterza.

Fedele, M., & Moini, G. (2006). Cooperare conviene? Intercomunalità e politiche pubbliche. *Rivista italiana di politiche pubbliche, 1*(1), 71–98. https://doi.org/10.1483/21754.

Ferrera, M. (1993). *Modelli di solidarietà: politiche e riforme sociali nelle democrazie*. Bologna: Il Mulino.

Ferrera, M. (1998). *Le trappole del welfare*. Bologna: Il Mulino.

Ferrera, M. (2008). Dal welfare state alle welfare regions: la riconfigurazione spaziale della protezione sociale in Europa. *La rivista delle politiche sociali, 3*, 17–49.

Ferrera, M. (2020). Mass democracy, the welfare state and European integration: A neo-Weberian analysis. *European Journal of Social Theory, 23*(2), 165–183. https://doi.org/10.1177/1368431018779176.

Folta, T. B. (1998). Governance and uncertainty: The trade-off between administrative control and commitment. *Strategic Management Journal, 19*(11), 1007–1028. https://doi.org/10.1002/(SICI)1097-0266(1998110).

Fosti, G., Larenza, O., & Rotolo, A. (2012). *La programmazione sociale e socio sanitaria nelle reti interistituzionali: il caso Regione Lombardia. Rapporto Oasi 2012*. Milano: Egea.

Franzoni, F., & Anconelli, M. (2014). *La rete dei servizi alla persona. Dalla norma all'organizzazione*. Roma: Carocci.

Geldof, D. (1999). New activation policies: Promises and risks. In M. Heikkila (Ed.), *Linking welfare and work* (pp. 13–26). European foundation for the improvement of living and working conditions: Dublin.

Girotti, F. (2007). *Amministrazioni Pubbliche*. Roma: Carocci.

Gori, C. (Ed.). (2011). *Come cambia il welfare lombardo. Una valutazione delle politiche Regionali*. Maggioli: Rimini.

Gualdani, A. (2007). *I servizi sociali tra universalismo e selettività* (Vol. 8). Giuffrè Editore.

Gualini, E. (2006). The rescaling of governance in Europe: New spatial and institutional rationales. *European Planning Studies, 14*(7), 881–904. https://doi.org/10.1080/09654310500496255.

Gualmini, E., & Sacchi, A. (2016). Come combattere la povertà: tentativi di universalismo nel welfare state italiano. *Polis, 30*(3), 377–405.

Hemerijck, A. (2012). Two or three waves of welfare state transformation? In N. Morel, B. Palier, & J. Palme (Eds.), *Towards a social investment welfare state?* (pp. 33–60). Chicago: The University of Chicago Press.

Hooghe, L., & Marks, G. (2001). *Multilevel governance and European integration*. Boulder: Rowman and Littlefield.

Jenson, J., & Saint-Martin, D. (2003). New routes to social cohesion? Citizenship and the social investment state. *Canadian Journal of Sociology/Cahiers canadiens de sociologie, 28*(1), 77–99. https://doi.org/10.2307/3341876.

Jung, T. (2010). Citizens, co-producers, customers, clients, captives? A critical review of consumerism and public services. *Public Management Review, 12*(3), 439–446. https://doi.org/10.1080/14719031003787940.

Kazepov, Y. (2008). The subsidiarization of social policies: Actors, processes and impacts. *European Societies, 10*(2), 247–273. https://doi.org/10.1080/14616690701835337.

Kazepov, Y. (Ed.). (2010). *Rescaling social policies: Towards multilevel governance in Europe*. Ashgate Publishing, Ltd..

Kazepov, Y., & Barberis, E. (2013). *Il welfare frammentato. Le articolazioni regionali delle politiche sociali italiane*. Carocci: Roma.

Kazepov, Y., & Sabatinelli, S. (2005). *Integrated approaches to active welfare and employment policies: Italy*. European Foundation for the Improvement of Living and Working Condition: Dublin.

Klijn, E. H., & Koppenjan, J. F. (2000). Public management and policy networks: Foundations of a network approach to governance. *Public Management an International Journal of Research and Theory, 2*(2), 135–158. https://doi.org/10.1080/14719030000000007.

Klok, P. J., Denters, B., Boogers, M., & Sanders, M. (2018). Intermunicipal cooperation in the Netherlands: The costs and the effectiveness of polycentric regional governance. *Public Administration Review, 78*(4), 527–536. https://doi.org/10.1111/puar.12931.

Kreuter, M. W., & Lezin, N. (2002). Social capital theory. Emerging theories in health promotion practice and research: Strategies for improving public health, 15, 228.

Le Grand, J. (2007). *The other invisible hand: Delivering public services through choice and competition*. Princeton: Princeton University Press.

Le Grand, J. (2011). Quasi-market versus state provision of public services: Some ethical considerations. *Public Reason, 3*(2), 80–89.

Lecy, J. D., Mergel, I. A., & Schmitz, H. P. (2014). Networks in public administration: Current scholarship in review. *Public Management Review, 16*(5), 643–665. https://doi.org/10.1080/14719037.2012.743577.

Madama, I. (2013). Beyond continuity? Italian social assistance policies between institutional opportunities and agency. *International Journal of Social Welfare, 22*(1), 58–68. https://doi.org/10.1111/j.1468-2397.2011.00835.x.

Madama, I. (2019). La politica socioassistenziale. In Ferrera, M. (a cura di), *Le politiche sociali*. Bologna: Il Mulino.

Martelli, A. (2006). *La regolazione locale delle politiche sociali. Un percorso d'analisi*. Milano: Franco Angeli.

Milio, S. (2014). The conflicting effects of multi-level governance and the partnership principle: Evidence from the Italian experience. *European Urban and Regional Studies, 21*(4), 384–397. https://doi.org/10.1177/0969776413493631.

Morel, N., Palier, B., & Palme, J. (2012). Beyond the welfare state as we know it? In N. Morel, B. Palier, & J. Palme (Eds.), *Towards a social investment welfare state?* (pp. 1–33). Chicago: The University of Chicago Press.

Nikolai, R. (2012). Towards social investment? Patterns of public policy in the OECD world. In N. Morel, B. Palier, & J. Palme (Eds.), *Towards a social investment welfare state?* (Vol. 91, p. 116). Chicago: The University of Chicago Press.

Ponzo, I. (2014). *Il welfare di comunità applicato alla cura.* Paper presented at the ESPANET Conference, Torino, 2014.

Powell, M., & Barrientos, A. (2004). Welfare regimes and the welfare mix. *European Journal of Political Research, 43*(1), 83–105. https://doi.org/10.1111/j.1475-6765.2004.00146.x.

Previtali, P. (2015). The Italian administrative reform of small municipalities: State-of-the-art and perspectives. *Public Administration Quarterly,* 548–568.

Previtali, P., & Favini, P. (2015). *Welfare locale tra continuità e innovazione: i servizi prima infanzia in provincia di Pavia.* Pavia University Press.

Previtali, P., & Favini, P. (2016). *L'organizzazione dei Piani di Zona in provincia di Pavia.* Pavia University Press.

Previtali, P., & Salvati, E. (2016). Governance e Performance nel Welfare Locale. Un'Analisi dei Piani di Zona della Provincia di Pavia. *Economia Aziendale Online, 7*(1), 1–15. https://doi.org/10.6092/2038-5498/7.1.1-15.

Previtali, P., & Salvati, E. (2019). Social planning and local welfare. the experience of the italian area social plan. *International Planning Studies, 24*(2), 180–194. https://doi.org/10.1080/135 63475.2018.1528864.

Ranci, C. (2006). Welfare locale, decentramento e cittadinanza. *La Rivista della Politiche Sociali, 1,* 127–135.

Salamon, L. (2012). Subsidiarity and the new governance: Reflections on the Lombard experience. In A. Colombo (Ed.), *Subsidiarity Governance. Theoretical and empirical models* (pp. 18–30). New York: Palgrave.

Salvati, E. (2016a). L'evoluzione della pianificazione zonale. Il caso dei Piani di Zona in Regione Lombardia. *Autonomie locali e servizi sociali, 39*(3), 499–514. https://doi.org/10.1447/85715.

Salvati, E. (2016b). Governance e organizzazione dei nove Piani di Zona della provincia di Pavia. Un'analisi comparata. In P. Previtali & P. Favini (Eds.), *L'organizzazione dei Piani di Zona in provincia di Pavia* (pp. 119–170). Pavia: Pavia University Press.

Salvati, E. (2020). Riorganizzare il welfare locale. Il modello del governance network e l'esperienza dei Piani di Zona lombardi. *Studi Organizzativi, 1,* 67–92. https://doi.org/10.3280/SO2020-001003.

Teles, F. (2016). *Local governance and intermunicipal cooperation.* Springer.

Teles, F., & Swianiewicz, P. (2018). Motives for revisiting inter-municipal cooperation. In F. Teles (Ed.), *Inter-municipal cooperation in Europe* (pp. 1–13). Palgrave Macmillan.

Trigilia, C. (2005). *Sviluppo locale. Un progetto per l'Italia.* Roma-Bari: Laterza.

Valkenburg, B. (2007). Individualising activation services: Thrashing out an ambiguous concept. In R. Van Berkel & B. Valkenburg (Eds.), *Making it personal.* Bristol: Policy Press.

van Popering-Verkerk, J., & van Buuren, A. (2016). Decision-making patterns in multilevel governance: The contribution of informal and procedural interactions to significant multilevel decisions. *Public Management Review, 18*(7), 951–971. https://doi.org/10.1080/14719037.2015.1 028974.

Chapter 3
A (Possible) Answer to Fragmentation in Social Assistance Policy. The Local Area Plan

Abstract The national Law No. 328 aimed for the first time to create a common national framework for social policies, through the creation of an innovative organisational arrangement for the local management of social-assistance interventions (the Local Area Plan). Such novelty has been framed as an organizational answer to the endemic fragmentation which affected the system of social services provision. This chapter will define what a Local Area Plan effectively is; how it is structured and what are its competencies, underlining strengths and weaknesses. From the dialogue between the literature concerning inter-municipal cooperation and Local Area Plans we will try to define the peculiarities of the Local Area Plan as an organisational instrument for boosting agreements between municipalities and providing different shaped social services. This effort will allow us to provide a theoretical framework that will serve to interpret the Local Area Plan's role and the elements that pertain to the greater or lesser propensity of this governance instrument to change.

Keywords Fragmentation · Local area plan · Public services' organization · Intermunicipal cooperation · Policy making · Local governance

3.1 Introduction

As we saw in the previous chapter, the national Law No. 328 aimed for the first time to create a common national framework for social policies. In order to achieve this goal, the law set the definition of an innovative organisational arrangement for the local management of social-assistance interventions – the Local Area Plan -, which give to municipalities the opportunity to jointly manage social services through an intermunicipal form of cooperation. With this expression we refer to specific "features of governance arrangements and institutions created to generate and maintain collaborative settings between different local governments in a particular territory" (Teles and Swianiewicz 2018, p.1).

For social services, these arrangements allowed to reframe the responsibilities of the public actor on the territory, enforce the benefits of economies of scale and

P. Previtali, E. Salvati, *Local Welfare and the Organization of Social Services*,
https://doi.org/10.1007/978-3-030-66128-1_3

redefine its relationship with the private sector opening the policy making process to the active participation of profit and non-profit associations and citizens (Bel and Warner 2016; Previtali and Favini 2015).

Despite the fact that part of the provisions stated in the law have been neglected, one fundamental element has come into being in all the regions, even if with different organisational models and competencies: the *Local Area Plan*.

Local Area Plans were introduced as an enforced model of governance founded on the need to drastically improve inter-municipal cooperation in the sector of social services provision (Bifulco 2008). From this point of view they had – and still have – the mission of solving organisational and governance problems (fragmentation, lack of effectiveness, scarce inclination for social innovation etc.) by improving horizontal (and multilevel, if needed) coordination (Kazepov 2010; Hovik and Hanssen 2015). In this work we refer to coordination initiative as "any reform (*or action*) carried out by the administration or delivery of benefits and services that explicitly aims at tackling fragmentation" (Champion and Bonoli 2011, p. 324). Such coordination, as stated by Champion and Bonoli, can range from guidelines for collaboration to initiatives aimed at merging two or more agencies. Despite the substantial differences, the overall aim is to change the models by which policies and services are planned and delivered (Borghi and Van Berkel 2007).

The need to improve cooperation and create new instruments for coordination (Salvati 2020), has been fuelled by the ever increasing presence of private actors in the supply chain of social services, in a context characterised by the end of the predominance of the bureaucratic hierarchical structure based on the centrality of the public sector, in favour of a more informal model of decision making that relies on "light" structures of governance and the centrality of private actors (both profit and non-profit) (Peters 1998; Haveri 2006; Kazepov 2010).

From this point of view the public actor is becoming more and more involved in building cooperation and partnerships with social actors, the Third Sector and other local authorities in order to produce new services, by employing a course of action that is defined as structured interaction or the building of governance networks (Haveri 2006; McGuire and Agranoff 2011; Previtali and Salvati 2019; Salvati 2020). This perfectly fits the actual functioning of the delivery of social services in Italy through the role of the Local Area Plan (Previtali and Favini 2016).

This chapter will look at what in effect a Local Area Plan is; how it is structured and what are its competencies. From the dialogue between the literature concerning inter-municipal cooperation and Local Area Plans we will try to define the peculiarities of the Local Area Plan as an organisational instrument for boosting agreements between municipalities and providing different shaped social services. Finally a theoretical framework will be presented that will serve to interpret the Local Area Plan's role and the elements that pertain to the greater or lesser propensity of this governance instrument to change.

3.2   The *Local Area Plan* as a New Organisational Instrument

Local Area Plans are organisational arrangements used to institutionalise and stabilise cooperation among municipalities for the provision of social services.[1] The Law No. 328/2000 stated that Italian municipalities must form inter-municipal groupings, which are "the instruments for the associated planning of services and social interventions of municipalities able to match their resources, and respond to needs, within a limited territorial area" (Previtali and Salvati 2019, 4). These inter-municipal networks are responsible for the supply of a great part of the social services provided by municipalities, in particular for small and medium size municipalities which wouldn't otherwise be able to supply those services both because of economic and organisational limitations.

The Local Area Plan can be conceived as a governance arena (Salvati 2016b) in which territorial actors are called upon to contribute to the process of policy production based – at least in the original idea – on the continuous flow of ideas and resources which should characterise a dynamic process of political production. From this point of view some specific and general tasks can be associated with the Local Area Plan:

- the definition of a territorial area within which to organise the services planning and supply
- making an individual's access to social services a vested/substantial right (*diritto esigibile*);
- recognising and institutionalising the presence of new actors within the social services network (how to regulate the relationship between public administration and private actors, broader cooperation, models for the accreditation process etc.);
- evaluating and adopting good practices (both for management and services supply);
- creating organisational instruments useful for fostering cooperation among municipalities (and other actors of the network) and concretely curbing fragmentation in the provision of social services.

According to what is stated in the national Law No. 328, the subjects who participate – with various duties and competences – in the life of the Local Area Plan are: municipalities, former territorial healthcare agencies (*Azienda Sanitaria Locale* – ASL), non-profit organisations, cooperation bodies, associations and bodies of social promotion, foundations and patronage bodies, and voluntary organisations. The increase in the number of actors involved from a governance perspective is a peculiar feature of this law, which aimed to reshuffle power and competencies in the social assistance sector by opening up local political production to the active participatory presence of a plurality of stakeholders. Obviously, a high number of

---

[1] In Italy, municipalities have the full and exclusive competence for the management and the supply of social services, keeping per se the so called *funzione sociale* (social function)

members which participate to the governance network, make even more complex its management, its effective coordination and require a solid level of trust among all the involved partners (Klijn et al. 2010).

Those in charge of providing a minimum unitary framework in the territory are the regional governments that, after the approbation of the 2001 constitutional reform, have gained exclusive competencies on the governance of social services (Bifulco 2008). The relationship that occurs between regional government and the Local Area Plans vary from region to region, ranging from a top-down model in which the Local Area Plans have reduced autonomy, like in the Veneto experience, to those in which there is a more dialectical relationship and an accentuated autonomy like in Emilia-Romagna and Lombardia, where the Regional government produces general guidelines for the definition of social priorities on which Local Area Plans have to operate.

The Law No. 328, Art. 8 prescribes that the regions determine territorial areas, modalities and tools for the *"unitary management of the local system of social networking services. In determining the territorial areas, the regions provide incentives in favour of the associated exercise of social functions "*. In particular, this Article also states what the boundaries of the Local Area Plan should overlap with those of the healthcare district.

This provision, which aimed to support the integration between the social and healthcare dimensions, has not been applied by all the regions; for example, in the RL there is a clear cut distinction between the healthcare district and the Local Area Plan area, which is in charge of social services. A distinction that has unavoidably fuelled territorial and functional fragmentation, and made successive attempts to piece together this fragmentation, if not completely unrealistic, at least extremely complicated. This still represents one of the main shortcomings in the Lombardy region welfare state system.

The Local Area Plan is constituted through the definition of a social planning document that must be approved by the Assembly of Mayors of the Municipalities related to the involved Territorial Area. This means that this arena of governance – at least in its original phase and in its minimal interpretation – is first of all defined in its boundaries by the planning choices of the municipalities involved in this agreement, which can enlarge or restrict the scopes of the cooperation.

It has (normally) a duration of 3 years and is legally established by a programme agreement (*accordo di programma* – AP). A programme agreement, in Italian administrative law, is an agreement between local authorities and public administrations through which the parties coordinate their activities for the realisation of services, interventions or the joint management of functions. In addition to the list of members, the AP also indicates which municipality is in charge of leading the association agreement and is administratively and financially responsible for the Local Area Plan (the so called *Ente capofila*), identifies the planning office (whether it is located within the *Ente capofila* or in an external structure such as a special company), and outlines the tasks of the *Ufficio di Piano*, the macro objectives of the plan, and the governance structure. So, the essential elements of the Local Area Plan's governance, within the programme agreement are:

- the municipality that leads the Local Area Plan;
- the Planning Office in charge of supporting the implementation of the Local Area Plan,
- the eventual presence of an external structure in charge to supply the social services defined by the Area Local Plan.

The programme agreement embodies the fundamental instrument for boosting coordination between different municipal administrations, in particular as regards the planning and the implementation of interventions which involve multiple levels of government and a plurality of actors, and is an attempt to curb the limitations of the municipalities' individual competences. The Local Area Plan was conceived as a tool to boost vertical (between the central, regional and municipal levels of government) and horizontal (between administrations, and between administrations and territorial actors) integration mechanisms (Bifulco 2010). In spite of this, its implementation on a highly fragmented basis has complicated the connection with the higher levels of government and has fragmented relationships with the social actors of the territory.

As far as the organisational features are concerned, if we look at the various territorial experiences in the Italian regions over the years we can find different governance arrangements and an overall picture which shows great variety in Local Area Plan arrangements (Bifulco and Centemeri 2008).

Despite this array of combinations (which would be complicated and not relevant to summarise here), we can find some invariant elements in the Local Area Plans organisational models (Salvati 2016). At the heart of the Local Area Plans there is the so called *Ufficio di Piano* (Planning office – UdP), which is responsible for the technical direction of the Local Area Plan policies and actions. The UdP provides technical support and manages the implementation processes of the planning phase, with particular reference to the tasks of piecing together and overcoming fragmentation, keeping the Local Area Plan's connection with societal actors, favouring access to services and promoting new welfare tools and actions. Of extreme importance is its exclusive competency of guaranteeing operational coordination between the various bodies of the Local Area Plan and the different actors and projects which operate in the territory. Furthermore, it defines and verifies the operational procedures for the implementation of the Programme Agreement (acting as the executive branch of the mayors' assembly), draws up progress reports for the municipalities and keeps the members informed on the progress of the implementation process of the *Ambito*.

The UdP is responsible for defining the social and welfare planning in a given territory, favouring coordination among the actors, assisting negotiation among the different subjects present on the territory, managing the budget, stimulating associated action among municipalities and therefore the inter-institutional coordination capacity and guaranteeing (theoretically) a leadership able to give coherence and continuity to the administrative action (Bifulco and Centemeri 2008; Bifulco 2016).

This role is integrated with the planning and orientation of developments and innovative and experimental actions. As such, it is easy to understand that the UdP plays a leading role within the Local Area Plan (Cataldi and Gargiulo 2010; Salvati 2016a), it represents the driving force behind the structure because all the decisions and planned actions pass necessarily through its scrutiny.

Independently from the UdP's role, the governance of the Local Area Plan is normally structured in two different ways: firstly, the organisational system may be based exclusively on the *Ufficio di Piano* that is organised within the social depart-ment[2] of the leading municipality and manages and plans social services without any form of externalisation, using the employees of the involved municipality(ies) to carry out the administrative tasks; or secondly, the production and provision of social services is in the hands of an *Azienda Speciale* (AS) that, in the Italian legal system, is a non-profit public company defined as an 'instrumental body' of the local authority with a legal character, entrepreneurial autonomy and its own statute, which has been approved by the municipal or provincial council or by the legislative body of an autonomous region or province. The *Azienda Speciale* has its own administrative and operative staff (psychologists, social workers, administrative staff, street level bureaucrats etc.) with its own budget that does not impinge on the budget of the partnered municipalities.

The main difference between the two solutions is the ability of the AS to act on the sector of public services supply with a more market oriented perspective and focus on efficiency, thus increasing the Local Area Plan capacity to act more quickly and independently, with all the risks and externalities associated with a process of "corporatisation". These outcomes can be hampered or exacerbated depending on whether the technical – political planning phase is embedded within the AS or if it is external and collocated within the leading municipality (*Ente capofila*). The sec-ond option avoids the merging of the planning and supply phases within a company that is outside of the municipality's administrative structure and, most of all, limits the risks that the political side (the *Assemblea dei sindaci*) lose control over the planning phase of social policy, weakening the representativeness and accountabil-ity dimensions of the policy cycle.

Hierarchically above the administrative structure, is the political leadership of the *Assemblea dei sindaci* which is an assembly composed of the mayors of the cit-ies (or their delegates) that are part of the inter-municipal agreement, and that is led by the *Presidente dell'Assemblea dei sindaci* (president of the mayors' assembly). The Assembly of Mayors is identified as the only political organ of the Local Area Plan and exercises a government function over the planning and supply phases. This body has a supervisory function and is responsible for defining the social policy strategies of the reference territory, the budget allocation and for controlling the technical implementation of the policies.

---

[2] Usually it is located within the *Ente capofila*, but it is not rare to see a division with one munici-pality as *Ente capofila* and another in charge of the *Ufficio di Piano*. This can be explained by two (not alternative) factors: a) a political division of the responsibilities/leading positions within the Local Area Plan, b) the presence of a municipality within the Local Area Plan that has a better equipped administrative sector (both in terms of human resources and operative skills).

Despite the role of the *Assemblea dei Sindaci*, substantially it is the UdP that coordinates the activities of the Local Area Plan and that assumes a function of technical direction capable of mobilising resources and guiding interventions, with the *Assemblea* holding the political leadership and a general supervision of policies. As far as the functioning of the Local Area Plan is concerned, the literature shows us how much they are subject to a process of strong "technicisation", which means that there is a preponderance of technicians over politicians when defining guidelines and objectives (Cataldi and Gargiulo 2010; Cataldi and Girotti 2012). This goes partially against the orientation at the basis of the constitution of the Local Area Plan, created by sanctioning the fundamental role of municipalities and politicians "in the establishment of decision-making arenas that combine the openness to the plurality of local bodies and actors with the recomposition of their partiality through cooperative agreements" (Bifulco 2010: 40).

The shift in the centre of gravity in favour of technicians and administrative personnel can be explained by three factors (Cataldi and Gargiulo 2010): the highly sectorial content of social policies; a much narrower model of participation compared to the constitutive premises of the Plans (Bifulco and Centemeri 2008); and, a steering function in which the bureaucratic part is strongly prominent, as an inevitable consequence of the (favourable) information asymmetry compared to the political side (Cataldi and Girotti 2012).

From this point of view, it is the model of governance adopted by the *Local Area Plan* itself that seems to strengthen the role of technicians (Cataldi and Gargiulo 2010; Salvati 2016a), with the devolution of resources and skills towards organisational tools such as the AS that often makes up for the structural weaknesses of municipalities. Despite the important role played by technicians, the role of politics should not however be considered completely marginal, given the ability of those in political leadership roles to "assert their ownership of planning processes by exercising, albeit ultimately, a binding and impassable power of veto" (Cataldi and Gargiulo 2010:22). So, for the sake of the empirical research, it is particularly interesting to inquire if the political part has a proactive role with the effective power to shape the policy agenda or if, ultimately, it has just a veto power to stop undesired outputs.

Alongside the UdP and the *Assemblea dei Sindaci*, there are another two arenas which structurally characterise the governance system of the Local Area Plan. The first is a restricted arena,[3] which usually carries out consultative and supporting functions delegated by the Assembly, formed of a restricted number of mayors and administrative staff, that has the duty of coordinating the work of the Local Area Plan, giving advice to the *Assemblea*, working on the main dossiers and supporting the mayors in taking the main decisions.

The second arena represents the institutionalised space in which the Third Sector and all of the social actors that operate in the Local Area Plan territory directly participate. This opportunity for citizens and associations to participate is one of the

---

[3] This arena is not codified and is not necessarily present in all the Local Area Plans

pillars of the Law No. 328/2000, which has among its aims the institutionalisation of open participation and the enforcement of transparency in the decision making process, which encourages collaboration with citizens (Bifulco and Centemeri 2008; Bifulco 2016). From this point of view the inception of the Local Area Plan represents a straightforward innovation because it views participation in the decision making process as an indispensable step for the improvement of local welfare. Local Area Plans are a paradigmatic case of "construction of organisational infrastructures for open and inclusive participation" (Bifulco 2016, p.15).

They therefore become, in the legislator's intentions, an instrument to push municipalities to govern the system of social welfare services in an associated and integrated way, with the aim of structurally involving citizens and the Third Sector (Bifulco 2010). A series of objectives that have not always been fully achieved during these years, shattering some of the hopes that have arisen with the birth of the Local Area Plan and producing mixed results (Bertin 2012; Bifulco 2016; Previtali and Salvati 2016). The persistent limitations of Local Area Plans efficiency are well summarised by Bifulco (2010) who identifies the main critical issues in three dimensions: shortcomings in the coordination between public and private actors, difficulties in the redistribution of decision-making power, and the kind of relationship that exists between politics and policies. From this point of view, the first two aspects, which contain elements concerning the governance and the model of structuring of the Local Area Plans' relationships, can explain – in part – the RL's successive regulatory intervention aimed at (attempting) strengthening the *Local Area Plan* by stimulating the definition of new borders and, indirectly, of new governance instruments.

Strictly in connection with the issue of public services delivery, administrative and governance fragmentation (Previtali 2015; Citroni et al. 2016), the literature has shown how the contextual presence of multiple governance relationships other than the Local Area Plan (mountain communities, associated management, unions of municipalities), make the production of innovative and effective policies more difficult and complicated (Previtali and Salvati 2019, p.13). This can be explained by the fact that: " a high number of well-established pre-existing relationships between municipalities could represent a disincentive to open up policy production to the participation of other social actors and to other types of partnership, especially of supra-area dimensions" (Previtali and Salvati 2019, p.13).

Over the last 30 years, due to the changes that occurred in Italy both to the welfare state and to the organisation of local government, the necessity to develop new instruments able to reconnect the different actors and resources "dispersed" within the system at different levels has grown drastically.

Needless to say, this situation is characterised by a high dispersion of authority which is fragmented among different levels, around which the governance issues are organised and managed (Hooghe and Marks 2001; van Popering-Verkerk and van Buuren 2016). This multilevel model is characterised by a network of formal and informal models of interactions, by a plurality of actors involved in decision making and in policy definition/implementation and, as a result of this state of affairs, by a structural condition of fragmentation (Citroni et al. 2016; van Popering-

Verkerk and van Buuren 2016; Previtali and Salvati 2019), which concerns actors, resources, powers, competences and knowledge. From this kind of model arise several questions which are particularly interesting both from a theoretical and empirical point of view: is there a new prominence of informal structure and interactions over the formal ones? Is it possible to define the optimal level/scale on which to take and implement decisions? Is there a peculiar model of interaction among formal and informal dimensions? Furthermore, and most interesting: is it possible to detect some conditions which can feed or conversely contain fragmentation?

All these questions – alongside others that lie outside the focus of this book – reveal how interesting it can be for researchers to investigate the organisational and political peculiarities of the Italian Local Area Plans, which were conceived as a possible answer to the organisational dilemma of a changing and evolving local welfare. What are the instruments available for understanding the functioning and development of the Local Area Plan? Which tools are useful for their analysis?

3.3   Different Approaches to the Study of *Local Area Plan*. A Proposal for a Theoretical Framework

To better understand the birth, the changes and the actual functioning of the Local Area Plan, we need a reliable theoretical framework to explain the role of this organisational instrument and its evolutionary trajectory. The definition of such a framework is not an easy task, due to the fact that the Local Area Plan lies at the intersection of different elements such as politics and political production, power and political authority, administrative behaviour and organization of public services, local government and local governance. A valuable framework should aim to keep all these elements within the equation, and avoid reducing this complex phenomenon to the analysis of a single element.

At the same time, we should be able to escape from a simple juxtaposition like the one between governance and government. If it is true that in the last few decades we have seen the overtaking of a decision making model exclusively based on the classical hierarchical structuration typical of administrative bureaucracy in favour of a more horizontal and informal model of planning and policy making, this does not mean, however, that political actors, bureaucrats and authority have been completely marginalised and have lost power in this renewed scenario (Peters and Pierre 2002).

The public actor now has a different role because it is called upon to act in a more complex environment, with multiple actors who are now able to exert pressure and influence over the multiple *loci* of the decision making, and so it has become increasingly committed to building partnerships and cooperation tools with the Third Sector, associations, private profit and other public authorities (Haveri 2006; McGuire and Agranoff 2011; Salvati 2016b).

As we have seen in the previous sections of this chapter, the Local Area Plan was created as an instrument useful for supporting the municipalities' planning capabilities and for framing a new governance model for social policy production based on associate management of particular competencies, pooling of previously dispersed resources, major transparency and the widespread participation of a plurality of social actors. It is particularly on the second aspect, citizens and groups participation, that a great bulk of the literature has concentrated its efforts in order to frame the novelty represented by the Local Area Plan and its new approach towards local welfare implementation (among others Bifulco and Centemeri 2008; Bifulco and Facchini 2013; Bifulco 2016). Despite the great importance of these studies for our understanding of the real and effective involvement of citizens and local actors in the planning and design of social policies, these studies cannot provide us with a comprehensive vision of the organisational processes and mechanisms on which Local Area Plans rely and, consequently, on the way the planning and supply of social services at the local level, really work.

A first interesting step in the direction of a more inclusive understanding of the role and functioning of the Local Area Plan is the one proposed by Cataldi and Gargiulo (2010) who apply to the experience of Piemonte's (another Italian region) Local Area Plans a systemic framework inspired by David Easton's theory. This framework examines the institutionalisation process of these arenas, by looking at the structuration of this model both from the internal side (the organisational model and the "borders" of the arena) and the external side (the relationship with the external environment, i.e. the social actors). This choice allows to inquire into the working dynamics of the input side (the relationship with social environment) from which derive part of the motivations/needs at the base of the policy making (an area under which the participatory dimension can also be placed) and of the output side, which pertains to the policies/measures/actions planned by the Local Area Plan. In the middle we have the "black box" that is the space in which the planning phase takes place and in which the policy decisions are shaped. Finally, this framework also enables – in a long term perspective – the evaluation of the policy outcomes, which represent the transformative impact that these social policies have on citizens and society.

This approach has been partially recalled by Previtali and Salvati (2019) in their analysis of the governance model of the Local Area Plans in the district of Pavia (located in the Lombardy Region). Here the authors attempted to define from a systemic perspective how the Local Area Plans have structured their organisation in order to enforce the relationship with social actors and give to the political side of the arena the opportunity to translate expressed social needs into policy decisions. The picture drawn is one in which Local Area Plans define institutionalised arenas of planning and decision in order to reduce disaggregation and fragmentation risks and the option of a "silent exit" by associate members. The authors present a model useful for exploring the relationship between governance structure and the performance of the Local Area Plan. In particular, the focus of attention is on the different governance's relationships with municipalities that are part of the same Local Area Plan. In summary, their research question is: under which circumstances is a Local

Area Plan more effective than another in reaching the planned goals? The model is built on two different variables: the first is the number of governance relationships within a territory (associated management of policy functions, unions of municipalities, territorial association, etc.) and the second the total number of involved municipalities.

Looking at the "administrative environment", Previtali and Salvati try to categorise the Local Area Plan according to the level of the municipalities' fragmentation and the number of extra Local Area Plan institutionalised cooperative relationships the municipalities, and members of the Local Area Plan, are involved in. This attempt, even if partial and focused only on a static dimension, places the Local Area Plan and its constitutive parts along with the institutional environment into context. The intersection of the two variables (Fig. 3.1) produces the following typology:

Loose relationship: Local Area Plans that have a high level of administrative fragmentation, with many municipalities and few institutionalised relationships. The Local Area Plan is the most advanced instrument of governance.

Network: Local Area Plans with many municipalities of which a large number are inserted into pre-existing institutional relationships. This arrangement defines a highly institutionalised network.

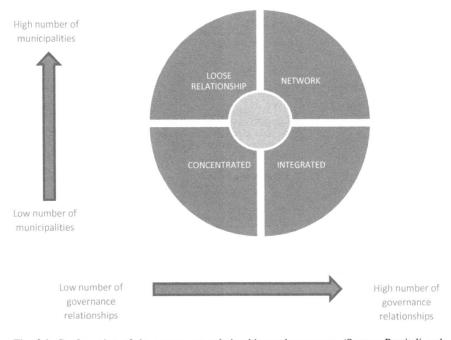

Fig. 3.1 Configuration of the governance relationships and structures. (Source: Previtali and Salvati (2019) Social planning and local welfare. The experience of the Italian area social plan, p.11)

Concentrated: Local Area Plans with both a low number of municipalities and inter-twined cooperation links.

Integrated: Local Area Plans composed of few municipalities with a high number of pre-existing relationships of institutionalised governance.

This typology enables us to understand how the institutional governance net-works in a given territory are organised, and helps to clarify the policy networks that intertwine and mobilise resources within and through different arenas but that are often contiguous and act in proximity. The model used to carry out the inquiry is based on four variables (Fig. 3.2), namely: the demand side (social needs), the sup-ply side (structures which provide services), governance actors and relationships, and the performance of the system in terms of effectiveness and innovation.

As it is easy to see, the model works on a system logic like the one used by Cataldi and Girotti (2012), with some caveats. We have the input (social needs) and the output (the supply side composed of public and private actors, the kinds of part-nerships working on the territory and the different services), and at the centre we have the black box, that in Previtali and Salvati's research design is mainly focused on the governance and (partially) government aspects. All these elements contribute to defining a specific feature of the system which is the effectiveness of the plan-ning. This is a multidimensional indicator composed of three fundamental variables for understanding the function of the Local Area Plan: (a) the realisation of the planned goals; that is the ability of the Local Area Plan to avoid the risk of realising

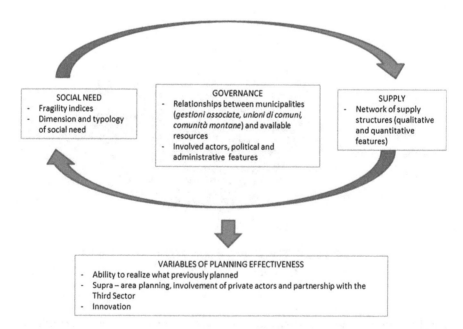

Fig. 3.2 Model of analysis of the effectiveness of social planning. (Source: Previtali and Salvati (2019) Social planning and local welfare. The experience of the Italian area social plan, p.6)

the planning phase as a goal *per se*, which leads to making a weak effort in the implementation of policy and approaching the planning as a "ceremony" (Meyer and Rowan 1977; Busso 2012), (b) the ability to create a network and boost coordination with the other actors of the network, through the presence of supra-area forms of collaboration, and, c) the capacity to innovate policies without a sort of path dependence occurring in the definition of the goals, that hamper the Local Area Plans' capacity to propose innovative policy answers to new social risks.

The three elements are connected and define aspects like the institutionalisation of the Local Area Plan, its openness to new ideas and innovation, its propensity to adopt social innovation and the ability to improve coordination (Salvati 2020). It is from the relationship that occurs between the three variables that the "performance of the system originates (...) and whose effectiveness can be seen in the use of the available resources and accomplishment of the goals defined in the social planning, in particular as regards all those tasks that could be considered innovative" (Previtali and Salvati 2019, 7).

Furthermore, reconstructing the various institutionalised governance relationships, whether they are Unions of Municipalities, Local Area Plans or Associated Managements, helps to understand the functioning of local government and the system of production and delivery of public policies during a period of accelerated decentralisation (Spalla 2005; Haveri 2006). Part of the development of local government and governance has been achieved through the institutionalisation of horizontal relationships, involving multiple actors and different institutions of territorial government (Lowndes and Skelcher 1998; Bolgherini et al. 2019). The public actors belonging to the same territory have begun to build, willingly or not, horizontal networks of governance based on particular relationships/models of collaboration and cooperation, placing the municipal authority at the centre of a new institutional network (Spalla 2005; Fedele and Moini 2006). This is precisely the very meaning of the concept of "network" and "institutions working in networks" – part of the neo-institutionalist reflection (March and Olsen 1989) – that is permeating local governance and government (Osborne and Baebler 1992; Rhodes 1997) and – as we will see later – also the Local Area Plan experience (Klijn and Koppenjan 2012; Salvati 2020).

These new institutional arrangements are useful for employing the scarce resources available to local authorities in a more efficient way and for containing the fragmentation of local government. To achieve this result in the social policy realm, it is necessary to promote a new model of local development and social cohesion, which stimulates better "planning of policies" to integrate and produce a harmonisation between the actions of the different actors (Salvati 2016a). At the heart of this process there is therefore the path of readjustment that local institutions and public administrations must follow, and their objectives, their organisational model and their rationality (Selznick 2011; March and Olsen 1989), as well as the need to proceed towards a paradigm shift, a readjustment of institutional practices and organisations.

Keeping as a benchmark a systemic approach for the analysis, Busso (2012) proposes a model for interpreting the organisation of the Local Area Plans and the arrangements of the relationships within and outside the Local Area Plan. Using a neo-institutionalist imprint, the model sketches the link that occurs between the values and principles at the base of the social planning within the Local Area Plan. These aspects directly influence: (a) the organisational field[4] defined by the actors in order to improve the planning phase, and (b) the capacity to keep closely in touch with the related territory and its social needs. These two elements together contribute to shaping the planning processes which influence the output of the planning effort. Positioned in an external position in the model we can find the pressure flow from outside that represents the exogenous factors which can affect the various trends in the resulting policies (Busso quotes, among others, the socio-economic aspects or peculiarities of a given territory).

Despite the other contributions, this model does not directly connect the input/demand side with the output and outcome dimension, thus overshadowing the direct relationship which has a heavy effect on the way in which Local Area Plans manage the planning of social services, their implementation and – eventually – their correction in case of under efficient/effective performances.

As in the Previtali and Salvati study on the role of the organisational field or governance/government relationships, it is essential to understand not only the organisational model but especially the different relationships that occur within these fields, how stable, routinized and institutionalised they are and how this whole aspect influences performance in the planning/supply of social services. Similarly to Salvati (2020), Busso and Negri (2012) underline how the changes in the normative landscape and the redefinition of power and authority arrangements, have put the Local Area Plans' work in a context of multilevel governance which did not only reshape the relationships among different levels of government, but opened the planning of social services to different actors, located on different steps of the power/authority ladder. This structural shift had direct consequences on the arrangement of the organisational field, on the values at the base of the planning phase, on the relationship with the territory and on the policy making process.

Another attempt to define a theoretical framework with the heuristic capacity to explain the Local Area Plan experience was made by Salvati (2020) in his study focused on the RL experience. The author uses the concept of network to explain the changes and evolution of the Local Area Plans in the last decade. The network model implies a series of stabilised relationships of a non-hierarchical nature, characterised by a strong interdependence between different actors, who share common interests with regard to certain policies or objectives and, in order to achieve these goals successfully, share their resources by recognising cooperation and coordination as the best ways to achieve the desired results (Börzel 1998; Klijn and Koppenjan 2012). At the heart of this concept there is the idea that actors need to improve and stabilise cooperation in order to boost security and stability in a disarticulated arena composed of several actors that are not always keen to make this cooperation per-

---

[4] The concept used by Busso is borrowed from the study of Dimaggio and Powell (1983) concerning sets of organisations that, together, constitute a recognised area of institutional life and the issue of organisational isomorphism.

manent. The interactions within the network are structured and stabilised as the result of a cumulative effect of cooperative relationships and games between the partners which over time define routinized lines of behaviour, and rules (both formal and informal), which determine the space of interaction (Salvati 2020).

According to Klijn (1996) there are three conditions that lead to the success of a network: (a) the actors involved make their resources fully available; (b) all the actors become mutually dependent on the shared resources (and the sharing modalities); and, (c) the definition of the sharing modalities and the use of these resources leads to the institutionalisation of the network.

The network logic seems rather useful to explain the Local Area Plans' organisation and functions because it frames and explains the Local Area Plans' need to increase coordination and reduce fragmentation by applying an advanced system of inter-municipal cooperation (that represents a noteworthy progress compared to the simple associated management of functions) which stems in a peculiar way from the involvement of social actors. To this point we should also add the need to stimulate the stability of the relationships among partners, to strengthen the coordination power of the Local Area Plan and to depend increasingly on the pooling of previously scattered resources (Salvati 2020).

The last analysis is from Previtali and Salvati (2020). Here the aim of the study is to explain how municipalities try to define and guarantee new structures and effective models of cooperation able to bypass the traditional hierarchal organisation of authority. In particular the paper proposes a framework useful for understanding what the conditions that can lead to the success (or failure) of a process of governance reorganisation are. The authors identify four variables that are determinant for these outputs: structures (within which another three variables are comprised, political homophily, the presence of pre-existing relationships among involved actors and mutual trust), processes, actors, and political and administrative leadership roles. The level of success in a governance review heavily depends on the characteristics of these variables (presence/absence, intensity level, etc.) and the way in which they interact with one another.

This approach is particularly interesting because it focuses on the process of governance structures' adaptation and propensity for change, highlighting an interesting aspect for intermunicipal cooperation models that work in a field like the one of social assistance that is intrinsically dynamic, and for which immobilisation and path dependent answers are more of an issue than an option.

3.4   Which Framework for the Analysis?

As shown by the overview of different studies dedicated to the experience of Local Area Plans that have employed specific theoretical frameworks for the analysis, a fruitful heuristic choice is that of considering the Local Area Plan from a systemic point of view. The systemic approach connected to the idea of the organisational field, recognises the new role exerted by the instrument of the Local Area Plan which has gained, year after year, an ever more active role in the policy formation process, and defines a "field" of action within which different actors, resources and (social) needs dynamically contribute to the planning of local welfare (Cataldi and Gargiulo 2010; Previtali and Salvati 2019). Furthermore this organisational field, which is part of a broader system, has assumed the shape of a governance network, which puts at centre stage the aim to institutionalise the cooperation and the pooling of resources and has the goal of enforcing coordination among involved members (Busso and Negri 2012; Bifulco 2016; Salvati 2020). This does not mean that such a structured field homogenises actors' interests and peculiarities, but simply that it gives them instruments for cooperation by enforcing trust and coordination, and making the behaviour of the partners predictable. Moreover by choosing this approach we can keep different aspects in the equation like:

- the input dimension: All the demands and social needs to which the Local Area Plan and the municipalities should provide political answers. A subsector of which. is:

  - the relationship with the external environment: how the Local Area Plan relates to external actors that are not directly involved in the governance system – because the Local Area Plan's planning cannot be totally open and based on a free entry and exit, otherwise it would result impossible to find a working agreement and an effective coordination (Busso and Negri 2012; Salvati 2020) – and defines how to manage the pressure from exogenous elements. The borders of the organisational field are obviously under major pressure during the planning phase, the moment in which the policies are decided.
- the ideational dimension: the principles (value, cultural, organisational, political etc.) that drive the choices made by the Local Area Plans;
- the governance/government dimension (the organisational field): how the Local Area Plans organise, the (eventual) strength of the network model, under which circumstances they choose a certain path, how they react to changes and stimulus, the relationships among the involved actors, how they manage and employ resources etc.;
- the output dimension: the policies/measures decided by the Local Area Plans, how the supply side is organised;
- the outcome dimension: the long term effects of these policies, how they impact on the reality in which the Local Area Plans act;
- the planning effectiveness: which gathers aspects from the output and outcome dimensions plus the Local Area Plans' capacity for innovation.

This model (Fig. 3.3) enables us to keep different aspects under control and provide the right consideration to all those features that are related to each other and contribute to shaping the organisation and the course of action of Local Area Plans. Such an intertwined model is fundamental to understanding the various directions from which pressure is exerted in order to modify/evolve the organisational field and its outputs/outcomes (Powell 1991). This pressure can hail from outside and be exerted both by social (i.e. Third Sector, associations etc.) and institutional actors

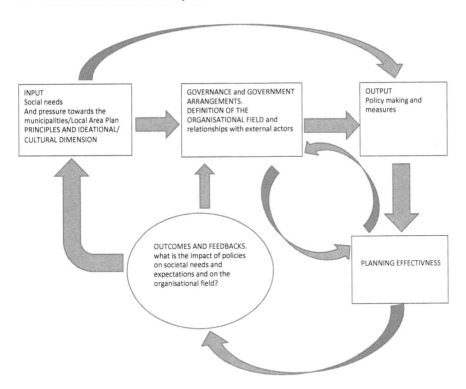

Fig. 3.3 *Local Area Plan*'s model of social planning (welfare development at local level)

(i.e. national and regional governments), but also from inside, by the partners that make up the Local Area Plan network and/or the actors that are part of the governance structure (i.e. other institutions, third sector, regional agencies etc.). The kinds of answers to the "pressure for change" differ from case to case according to: the network's ability to adapt itself to new challenges, the capacity of leadership to steer the network within a path of change, the level of trust among members and the presence of norms (formal and informal) able to provide the right tools for an effective change.

As stated in the introduction we will focus on a particular case in the Italian context – the one of the *Regione Lombardia* – and we are mainly interested in looking at how Local Area Plans reacted to an external shock (a reform proposal which involved the governance and the organisation of the Local Area Plans), both from the organisational side and the output side. The changes in these two dimensions have obvious repercussions on all the other aspects that define the Local Area Plans' "system" too.

In order to improve the heuristic potential of our theoretical framework, we also need to take into consideration the fact that the Local Area Plans act in a frame characterised by a high level of fragmentation and in a context of social services provision mainly based on the principle of territorialisation. This process aims to bring social services and welfare provisions as close as possible to citizens, enforcing the effectiveness and the personalisation of the services, to cope better with new social issues (Andreotti et al. 2012; Salvati 2016a; Previtali and Salvati 2019).

Such a process is strictly connected to the transformations now occurring to the organisation of local government/governance models and to the new competencies attributed to local actors (public and private) (Rhodes 1997; Peters 1998). As stated by Haveri (2006, 33) local governance is a concept which defines '(…) the many changes that can be seen in the way municipalities and other local-level actors solve problems and respond to societal challenges at local level'. What is actually being sought by actors, is the definition and guarantee of a new effective model of cooperation, able to by-pass the traditional hierarchal organisation of authority (Haveri 2006; Previtali and Salvati 2020).

In as much as we are interested in understanding the way in which a Local Area Plan reacts to external pressure for change, and in trying to understand which factors can explain failure or success in this process, we focus our attention on the central box of our scheme, the one dedicated to the arrangements of the organisational field (Fig. 3.3). This is particularly important because this is a missing piece in the puzzle of our knowledge of the Local Area Plan's reality, as underlined in the literature review. How does a flexible but institutionalised arena, focused on a specific sector of action, based on linkages of trust and mutual dependence, react to pressure for change? We are aware that our research is not exhaustive in terms of these organisational, institutional and political issues but we think that it can contribute to better grasping what happens in the "black box" of inter-municipal cooperation in a phase of (potential) change.

That said, we need to find some useful variables to employ in our empirical research. According to these premises, in the model developed by Previtali and Salvati (2020) for detecting the paths of local governance change, we can find some useful hints provided by their analysis on the implementation of the governance of collaborations based on inter-municipal cooperation. As stated before, the authors distinguished some indicators: structures (divided between size and number of municipalities, the type of previous ties, the level of trust and the political relationships among actors), processes, actors, the group of barriers that tend to obstacle local governance and the paradoxes associated with inter-municipal collaboration.

These variables are extremely useful because they can be placed within the organisational dimension within our scheme, thus providing valuable indicators to explain why a process of collaboration and/or reform can encounter failure or success.

3.4.1 Structure

Structure is the system of ties and opportunities according to which actors – as part of a defined setting – can operate, and so influence the distribution of power and resources (a heavily unbalanced distribution instead of a– at least partially – balanced distribution, may lead to domination instead of cooperation), the agenda setting i.e. the process of making public issues an actionable government priority (Zahariadis 2016), and the decision making models (Vangen et al. 2015; Previtali and Salvati 2020). The structure arrangements can be understood by identifying who the involved actors are, how they relate to one another and what the models of interconnection are. Furthermore the structure is determined – especially in a context of inter-municipal cooperation – by the level of power delegation and the pooling of resources accepted by all the partners (Salvati 2020).

The structure is what influences the capacity to find balance between efficiency and inclusiveness (Verweij et al. 2013), this means the capacity to have a structure tight enough to be consensus oriented in its decision making style, but that is able to have a process widely open to the contributions of various and different actors, according to the goals at stake. In order to improve a model of collaborative governance, these organisational arrangements are built upon the need to support the development of horizontal relationships between actors, instead of vertical links, so shifting the process towards horizontal coordination, which allows adaptation in order to cope with territorial needs and better coordination of the efforts of the various actors collocated at the same level (Hanssen et al. 2013; Vangen et al. 2015).

When we talk about structure in connection with the theme of inter-municipal cooperation, we essentially refer to elements like the number and size of municipalities, the role and political orientation of mayors and city counsellors, and the complexity of the relationships among the actors.

A certain strain of literature considers complexity a good feature because it implies a certain variety in the structure which allows for the provision of different solutions to various problems, an asset which is of particular relevance when we refer to the production of services (Oakerson 1999; Klok et al. 2018). A complex and fragmented system also offers the opportunity to mobilise different resources and to rely more on a system of horizontal relationship in order to solve collective problems (Klok et al. 2018). An interesting question to ask is whether the complexity is based on a system of weak or strong ties. In the weak system, a high level of fragmentation is connected to the opportunity to support different types of interactions among actors, and in particular it enables "local governments to solve collective action dilemmas using horizontal networks" (Feiock 2007, 57). On the other hand a system based on strong ties presumes a more limited number of involved actors, with more structured and limited relationships that determine a closer network of cooperation. If networks with weak ties are theoretically more open to experiencing new collaboration models, in networks based on strong ties as stated by Klolk et al., there is the advantage of '(…) strong social control, and information to monitor non cooperative behaviour is easily available. This facilitates the development of mutual trust because the reputations of participants are at stake' (Klok et al. 2018, 530).

A second characterising element of structure complexity is the level of trust among network partners that can be affected by certain variables: whether it is easy or difficult to have free rider behaviour, if there is or not active cooperation among actors, how partners are embedded in the network organisational structure, if there is or not a safety valve that gives partners the opportunity to opt out in the case of dissents on certain decisions thus reducing the risk that conflicts become disruptive (Klok et al. 2018), if the benefits of cooperation are high and spread among participants and if partners recognise the benefits and the spillover effects of trustworthy arrangements (Silva et al. 2018).

The number and size of municipalities has an effect on the costs and benefits of cooperation because it involves both the resources that municipalities control and the power exerted by them, according to their size (Klok et al. 2018; Previtali and Salvati 2019). In a polycentric system of governance, in which there are multiple centres of authority and so a proliferation of fragmentation, the number and the size of municipalities involved in the governance network can deeply affect not only the network effectiveness but also its capability to reform itself in order to enforce the cooperation channel via new governance arrangements (Klok et al. 2018).

Literature tells us that small size municipalities are more prone to collaboration due to their lack of resources and limited capacity to provide services and that the level of embeddedness in networks helps to feed network trust (Klok et al. 2018). Despite this it may also be that small size municipalities are more reluctant to form a broader network if the new partners are for the large part big municipalities, and this it is due to the risk of perceived annexation. Furthermore the augmentation of complexity – number of cities and citizens – may be considered an obstacle to developing new types of collaborations. So, for our purposes, number and size can be measured as follows: the population of the municipalities (with particular attention to the number of citizens who live in small municipalities), and the ratio between large and small municipalities.

Another issue at stake, that is connected to the leadership variable, is the degree of political homophily within and among the network/s. With this concept we refer to the presence of political and ideological/value similarities among the network's participants which indicates the actors' inclination to enforce collaboration more frequently with those that share similar stances (Song et al. 2018). This variable is considered extremely important for boosting collaboration especially in extremely fragmented contexts where partisan aspects can be seen as fundamental to fostering new models of collaboration and reducing transaction costs (Gerber et al. 2013). This aspect is particularly important because it is the political leadership which in the end decides the network constitution, the degree of cooperation, the amount of shared resources and the common goals of the network: political similarities may make the cooperation easier and so influence the adoption of certain kinds of policies and implementations. Despite the scarcity of works on this specific topic, recent studies confirmed that the presence of political similarities lowers the transaction costs of collaboration and the risks of defection, so the likelihood of inter-network cooperation is enhanced (Song et al. 2018).

Political homophily can be measured by looking at which political party mayors and elected officials of networks belong to. It is possible to consider only the leadership roles in a network and/or all the mayors who adhere to a certain network: with the former we define the inter-network political homophily, with the latter the intra-network political homophily. According to the aims of this research, we will focus on the inter-network political homophily.

3.4.2 *Process*

The process aspect is connected to the way in which the coordination takes place, how actors behave, cooperate, communicate, make and implement decisions, share responsibilities and evaluate outcomes (Vangen et al. 2015; Previtali and Salvati 2020). The processual dimension is dynamic and can take different shapes, which relate to both formal and more informal linkages among actors, but that are all directed toward reaching the goal of improving inter-organisational collaborations (Previtali and Salvati 2020).

Needless to say, these processes take place in a framework characterised by a high dispersion of authority which is fragmented among different levels, around which the governance issues are organised and managed (Hooghe and Marks 2001; van Popering-Verkerk and van Buuren 2016). This multilevel governance model is characterised by a network of formal and informal models of interactions, by a plurality of actors involved in decision making and in policy implementation and, as a result of this condition, by a high level of fragmentation (van Popering-Verkerk and van Buuren 2016; Previtali and Salvati 2019). The changes occurring to governance models are showing us that it is especially the interplay between informal and procedural interactions that best explains the dynamics and the decision-making outputs in governance networks (Edelenbos and Klijn 2007; Koch 2013; van Popering-Verkerk and van Buuren 2016). The attention payed to the unstructured interactions among actors that do not follow formal procedure or institutional proceeding but that gather together partners who have a common goal, are labelled as interactive governance (Torfing et al. 2012; Sørensen 2013).

These non-formalised and soft features are peculiar elements of these new governance networks, and shed a light on the importance of factors like trust, collaboration, and the absence of opportunistic behaviour which has an influence over the performance of governance networks: better outcomes can be achieved within network settings characterised by the presence of these soft and informal assets (Sørensen and Torfing 2009).

In this framework, inter-organisational collaboration is the product of 'efficiency-improving and disruption-resolving which are the efforts of stakeholders achieving common goals' (Song et al. 2018), p.262). Collaboration mainly pertains to the elements that affect the day to day work of inter-organisational arrangements and their ability to ensure cooperation via collaborative benefits (Vangen et al. 2015). In a situation of elevated fragmentation the main response to solving this problem is coordination, a goal that is quite impossible to achieve without effective collaboration, which can be encouraged by various reasons: instrumental, ideological/value, participatory etc. (Vangen et al. 2015). One variable that can be used to measure the propensity for collaboration is to examine the previous working relationships among the individual officers involved in the management of the organisations (especially the top and middle level bureaucrats who lead the networks day by day): was there already a tendency to cooperate among the networks in some areas? Were the officers accustomed to working together?

If the answers are positive, it means that it would be much easier to build a model of cooperation based on collaborative governance, and push forward towards closer inter-organisational coordination (Huxham et al. 2000; Vangen et al. 2015; Crosby et al. 2017).

3.4.3   Actors

When we refer to actors within a governance network, we refer to a wide array of subjects which includes both institutional and non-institutional actors, politicians, bureaucrats, administrative staff, experts, citizens, associations, the third sector, profit and non-profit organisations etc. This variety perfectly summarises the multiplicity of actors within a governance network and so the fragmentation of relationships and interaction. Furthermore this heterogeneity finds a straightforward confirmation in the presence of power asymmetries that can pertain both to the organisational level of the network and the individual partners of a collaboration (Huxham et al. 2000). Obviously, collaboration activity within a network would be easier, if all the involved actors did not perceive a structural power asymmetry, but as correctly pointed out by Huxham this can be difficult to achieve if the organisations involved have different sizes or have aims which make the collaboration more important to one partner than another (Huxham 1991).

Differences in interests and informal relationships can frequently lead to collaboration that does not work in the expected manner, and that is why the presence of leadership able to foster trust and cooperation among actors is so important.

One way of trying to reduce to a minimum the level of uncertainty and so the risk of failure is, as underlined by Haveri (2006), the ability to create a diffuse political consensus among the actors of this change (for example if municipalities are involved, among mayors) and the presence of a political leadership able to unite the actors of a network and lead them towards a renewed model of governance. This type of integrative and transformative leadership (Crosby et al. 2017) should not be considered only as the effort of one-single-man in charge, but as the ability to orchestrate collaborative work by supporting innovation, promoting working cooperation and fruitfully exploiting diffused competencies and know how (Crosby et al. 2017). Conversely, a lack of politics and of leadership may produce more uncertainty among actors, leading to a sure failure in the reform process and making cooperation and coordination even more difficult and complicated. The presence or absence of a political leadership committed to obtaining a successful output of the reform can be considered an empirical instrument useful for measuring how much the uncertainty level is reduced in a certain context.

According to Crosby et al. (2017, 660–661) there are four leadership roles:

(a) Sponsors are actors such as mayors, legislators, or agency heads that can employ political authority as a resource to spend in order to boost collaboration and innovation and to remove barriers that may obstacle the achievement of those results;

(b) Champions are different from sponsors in that they do not have formal powers but base their actions on informal authority to support an organisation throughout a path of change and to enforce collaborative processes. Their resources are personal and professional skills, competences, and innovative ideas, valuable in enforcing the governance structure;

(c) Catalysts are committed to transformative learning and their main aim is to change the identity and goals of the people with whom they are working;

(d) Implementers are actors who apply new ideas and procedures in order to get things done and they intervene in particularly confused moments when the implementation of change seems difficult to achieve. Implementers foster new norms and organisational arrangements by introducing innovative ideas.

These four types can be simultaneously present or can intervene in different moments; these roles may be carried out by a single actor or by a group, depending on the different situations (Crosby et al. 2017).

Another important actor with the potential to change organisational inertia and lead to a governance change is the network orchestrator (Cristofoli et al. 2017). Bartelings et al. (2017) identified this figure as the one that can manage inter-organisational relationships with the aim of making them easier and more profitable by enforcing the exchanges between organisations, supporting and transferring knowledge, and are committed to 'field work' and so create a real 'bridge' between organisations. The definition provided by the author is extremely clear; it states that the orchestrational work is 'the role in which the orchestrator consciously integrates and therefore fine-tunes activities which have to be executed by network partners from various organisations to deliver concrete jointly arranged results' (Bartelings et al. 2017, 355). Even though the figure of the network orchestrator mainly refers to managers that work within organisations, thanks to our field experience we can say that this role is also suited to external personalities/experts who can act as facilitators in this process of network coordination, thus effectively carrying out the role of orchestrator in this passage of inter-organisational rearrangement. It is common for researchers or consultants to be commissioned to help in the managing of network collaborative working processes and provide support in the field (Vangen et al. 2015). Our research activity led us to collaborate closely with regional and municipal officers, involving us in the so-called 'field work' in order to facilitate the realisation and the implementation of the regional policy: this gave us the opportunity to directly collect precious and unique data in the field.

3.4.4   Barriers to Local Governance Change

During a process of organisational change or redefinition of collaborative interplay, the interaction between the 3 main factors, structures, processes and actors, can produce a series of barriers that can be an obstacle to successfully fulfilling the goal. Termeer identified a group of five barriers to local governance (Termeer 2009,

311–312): (1) conflicting convictions concerning good policy making, which mainly pertain to the possible tensions between old and new models of governance, and concern the redefinition of old process and organisational arrangements. Here the role that can be played by path dependence mechanisms, which can prevent any sort of change, is particularly evident; (2) stereotyping potential partners is the tension produced by the clash between the narrative of the 'newness' presented as intrinsically good and the reaction caused in the representatives of the old system: This clash can frequently contribute to locking in the system; (3) the framing of the situation pertains to the way in which the change opportunity is presented to actors and can put pressure on who has the task of implementing changes; (4) fear concerning the risk of failure; and, (5) cover-up strategies can hide difficulties and so limit the opportunity for actors to openly face problems and risks.

All these elements are essential to understanding the motivations at the base of a successful or unsuccessful policy disposition, especially if it concerns organisational and governance arrangements. The way in which these variables operate and interact in a defined context and the paths of interaction among them, define the structure of ties/opportunities in which policy implementation takes place. So, this provides a valuable indicator for our theoretical framework, one which is capable of gaining relevant empirical insights that can explain the trajectories taken by different actors.

This scheme will be used in the fourth chapter to analyse some successful experiences of Local Area Plans aggregation and redefinition, and will provide the opportunity to underline which elements can positively lead to successful governance reform (in the field of social policy).

References

Andreotti, A., Mingione, E., & Polizzi, E. (2012). Local welfare systems: A challenge for social cohesion. *Urban Studies, 49*(9), 1925–1940. https://doi.org/10.1177/0042098012444884.

Bartelings, J., Goedee, J., Raab, J., & Bijl, R. (2017). The nature of orchestrational work. *Public Management Review, 19*(3), 342–360. https://doi.org/10.1080/14719037.2016.1209233.

Bel, G., & Warner, M. E. (2016). Factors explaining inter-municipal cooperation in service delivery: A meta-regression analysis. *Journal of Economic Policy Reform, 19*(2), 91–115. https://doi.org/10.1080/17487870.2015.1100084.

Bertin, G. (Ed.). (2012). *Piani di zona e governo della rete*. Milano: FrancoAngeli.

Bifulco, L. (2008). Politiche pubbliche e partecipazione. Alcune piste per la comparazione fra Italia e Franca. *Rivista italiana di politiche pubbliche, 3*(2), 65–91. https://doi.org/10.1483/27437.

Bifulco, L. (2010). Strumenti per la programmazione negoziale. I Piani sociali di zona ei Contratti di quartiere. *Rivista italiana di politiche pubbliche*, (2), 31–57. https://doi.org/10.1483/32672.

Bifulco, L. (2016). Citizenship and governance at a time of territorialization: The Italian local welfare between innovation and fragmentation. *European Urban and Regional Studies, 23*(4), 628–644. https://doi.org/10.1177/0969776414531969.

Bifulco, L., & Centemeri, L. (2008). Governance and participation in local welfare: The case of the Italian Piani di Zona. *Social Policy & Administration, 42*(3), 211–227. https://doi.org/10.1111/j.1467-9515.2007.00593.x.

Bifulco, L., & Facchini, C. (2013). *Partecipazione sociale e competenze. Il ruolo delle professioni nei Piani di Zona*. Milano: FrancoAngeli.

Bolgherini, S., Dallara, C., & Profeti, S. (2019). A shallow rationalisation?'Merger mania' and side-effects in the reorganisation of public-service delivery. *Contemporary Italian Politics, 11*(2), 112–136. https://doi.org/10.1080/23248823.2019.1603650.

Borghi, V., & Van Berkel, R. (2007). New modes of governance in Italy and the Netherlands: The case of activation policies. *Public Administration, 85*(1), 83–101. https://doi.org/10.1111/j.1467-9299.2007.00635.x.

Börzel, T. A. (1998). Organizing Babylon-on the different conceptions of policy networks. *Public Administration, 76*(2), 253–273. https://doi.org/10.1111/1467-9299.00100.

Busso, S. (2012). Conclusione. In N. Busso & N. Negri (Eds.), *La programmazione sociale a livello zonale. Innovazione, tradizione, rituali*. Roma: Carocci.

Busso, N., & Negri, N. (Eds.). (2012). *La programmazione sociale a livello zonale. Innovazione, tradizione, rituali*. Roma: Carocci.

Cataldi, L., & Gargiulo, E. (2010). VIII. I Piani di zona nella Provincia di Torino tra percorsi di istituzionalizzazione, veti politici e imperativi tecnici. *Autonomie locali e servizi sociali, 33*(3), 403–420. https://doi.org/10.1447/34357.

Cataldi, L., & Girotti, F. (2012). Dentro la scatola nera dei processi di pianificazione zonale. Modelli di gestione, prospettive di istituzionalizzazione e arene di potere. *Autonomie locali e servizi sociali, 35*(2), 199–218. https://doi.org/10.1447/38937.

Champion, C., & Bonoli, G. (2011). Institutional fragmentation and coordination initiatives in western European welfare states. *Journal of European Social Policy, 21*(4), 323–334. https://doi.org/10.1177/0958928711412220.

Citroni, G., Lippi, A., & Profeti, S. (2016). Local public services in Italy: still fragmentation. In Public and Social Services in Europe, H. Wollmann, I. Koprić, & G. Marcou (Eds.), *Public and social services in Europe: From public and municipal to private sector provision* (pp. 103–117). London: Springer/Palgrave Macmillan.

Cristofoli, D., Meneguzzo, M., & Riccucci, N. (2017). Collaborative administration: The management of successful networks. *Public Management Review, 19*(3), 275–283. https://doi.org/10.1080/14719037.2016.1209236.

Crosby, B. C., 't Hart, P., & Torfing, J. (2017). Public value creation through collaborative innovation. *Public Management Review, 19*(5), 655–669. https://doi.org/10.1080/14719037.2016.1192165.

DiMaggio, P. J., & Powell, W. W. (1983). The iron cage revisited: Institutional isomorphism and collective rationality in organizational fields. *American Sociological Review, 48*, 147–160.

Edelenbos, J., & Klijn, E. H. (2007). Trust in complex decision-making networks: A theoretical and empirical exploration. *Administration & Society, 39*(1), 25–50. https://doi.org/10.1177/0095399706294460.

Fedele, M., & Moini, G. (2006). Cooperare conviene? Intercomunalità e politiche pubbliche. *Rivista italiana di politiche pubbliche, 1*(1), 71–98. https://doi.org/10.1483/21754.

Feiock, R. C. (2007). Rational choice and regional governance. *Journal of Urban Affairs, 29*(1), 47–63. https://doi.org/10.1111/j.1467-9906.2007.00322.x.

Gerber, E. R., Henry, A. D., & Lubell, M. (2013). Political homophily and collaboration in regional planning networks. *American Journal of Political Science, 57*(3), 598–610. https://doi.org/10.1111/ajps.12011.

Hanssen, G. S., Mydske, P. K., & Dahle, E. (2013). Multi-level coordination of climate change adaptation: By national hierarchical steering or by regional network governance? *Local Environment, 18*(8), 869–887. https://doi.org/10.1080/13549839.2012.738657.

Haveri, A. (2006). Complexity in local government change: Limits to rational reforming. *Public Management Review, 8*(1), 31–46. https://doi.org/10.1080/14719030500518667.

Hooghe, L., & Marks, G. (2001). *Multilevel governance and European integration*. Boulder: Rowman and Littlefield.

Hovik, S., & Hanssen, G. S. (2015). The impact of network management and complexity on multi-level coordination. *Public Administration, 93*(2), 506–523. https://doi.org/10.1111/padm.12135.

Huxham, C. (1991). Facilitating collaboration: Issues in multi-organizational group decision support in voluntary, informal collaborative settings. *Journal of the Operational Research Society, 42*(12), 1037–1045. https://doi.org/10.1057/jors.1991.198.

Huxham, C., Vangen, S., Huxham, C., & Eden, C. (2000). The challenge of collaborative governance. *Public Management an International Journal of Research and Theory, 2*(3), 337–358. https://doi.org/10.1080/14719030000000021.

Kazepov, Y. (Ed.). (2010). *Rescaling social policies: Towards multilevel governance in Europe.* Ashgate Publishing, Ltd..

Klijn, E. H. (1996). Analyzing and managing policy processes in complex networks: A theoretical examination of the concept policy network and its problems. *Administration & Society, 28*(1), 90–119. https://doi.org/10.1177/009539979602800104.

Klijn, E. H., & Koppenjan, J. (2012). Governance network theory: Past, present and future. *Policy & Politics, 40*(4), 587–606. https://doi.org/10.1332/030557312X655431.

Klijn, E. H., Edelenbos, J., & Steijn, B. (2010). Trust in governance networks: Its impacts on outcomes. *Administration & Society, 42*(2), 193–221. https://doi.org/10.1177/0095399710362716.

Klok, P. J., Denters, B., Boogers, M., & Sanders, M. (2018). Intermunicipal cooperation in the Netherlands: The costs and the effectiveness of polycentric regional governance. *Public Administration Review, 78*(4), 527–536. https://doi.org/10.1111/puar.12931.

Koch, P. (2013). Overestimating the shift from government to governance: Evidence from Swiss metropolitan areas. *Governance, 26*(3), 397–423. https://doi.org/10.1111/j.1468-0491.2012.01600.x.

Lowndes, V., & Skelcher, C. (1998). The dynamics of multi-organizational partnerships: An analysis of changing modes of governance. *Public Administration, 76*(2), 313–333. https://doi.org/10.1111/1467-9299.00103.

March, J., & Olsen, J. (1989). *Rediscovering institutions: The organizational basis of politics.* New York: Free Press.

McGuire, M., & Agranoff, R. (2011). The limitations of public management networks. *Public Administration, 89*(2), 265–284. https://doi.org/10.1111/j.1467-9299.2011.01917.x.

Meyer, J. W., & Rowan, B. (1977). Institutionalized organizations: Formal structure as myth and ceremony. *American Journal of Sociology, 83*(2), 340–363. https://doi.org/10.1086/226550.

Oakerson, R. J. (1999). *Governing local public economies: Creating the civic metropolis.* Ics Press.

Osborne, D., & Baebler, T. (1992). *Reinventing government: How the entrepreneurial spirit is transforming the public sector.* Reading, MA: Addison – Wesley.

Peters, B. (1998). Managing horizontal government: The politics of co-ordination. *Public Administration, 76*(2), 295–311. https://doi.org/10.1111/1467-9299.00102.

Peters, G. B., & Pierre, J. (2002). Multi-level governance: A view from the garbage can. *Manchester Papers in Politics: EPRU Series, 1*, 2002.

Powell, W. W. (1991). *Expanding the scope of institutional analysis.* Chicago: The university of Chicago Press.

Previtali, P. (2015). The Italian administrative reform of small municipalities: State-of-the-art and perspectives. *Public Administration Quarterly, 39*(4), 548–568.

Previtali, P., & Favini, P. (2015). *Welfare locale tra continuità e innovazione: i servizi prima infanzia in provincia di Pavia.* Pavia University Press.

Previtali, P., & Favini, P. (2016). *L'organizzazione dei Piani di Zona in provincia di Pavia.* Pavia University Press.

Previtali, P., & Salvati, E. (2016). Governance e Performance nel Welfare Locale. Un'Analisi dei Piani di Zona della Provincia di Pavia. *Economia Aziendale Online, 7*(1), 1–15. https://doi.org/10.6092/2038-5498/7.1.1-15.

Previtali, P., & Salvati, E. (2019). Social planning and local welfare. The experience of the Italian area social plan. *International Planning Studies, 24*(2), 180–194. https://doi.org/10.1080/13563475.2018.1528864.

Previtali, P. & Salvati, E. (2020). Area social plans and local governance of inter-organisational collaborations, forthcoming.

Rhodes, R. (1997). *Understanding governance*. Buckingham: Open University Press.

Salvati, E. (2016a). L'evoluzione della pianificazione zonale. Il caso dei Piani di Zona in Regione Lombardia. *Autonomie locali e servizi sociali, 39*(3), 499–514. https://doi.org/10.1447/85715.

Salvati, E. (2016b). Governance e organizzazione dei nove Piani di Zona della provincia di Pavia. Un'analisi comparata. In P. Previtali & P. Favini (Eds.), *L'organizzazione dei Piani di Zona in provincia di Pavia* (pp. 119–170). Pavia: Pavia University Press.

Salvati, E. (2020). Riorganizzare il welfare locale. Il modello del governance network e l'esperienza dei Piani di Zona lombardi. *Studi Organizzativi*, (1), 67–92. https://doi.org/10.3280/SO2020-001003.

Selznick, P. (2011). *Leadership in administration: A sociological interpretation*. Quid Pro Books.

Silva, P., Teles, F., & Ferreira, J. (2018). Intermunicipal cooperation: The quest for governance capacity? *International Review of Administrative Sciences, 84*(4), 619–638. https://doi.org/10.1177/0020852317740411.

Song, M., Park, H. J., & Jung, K. (2018). Do political similarities facilitate interlocal collaboration? *Public Administration Review, 78*(2), 261–269. https://doi.org/10.1111/puar.12887.

Sørensen, E. (2013). Institutionalizing interactive governance for democracy. *Critical Policy Studies, 7*(1), 72–86. https://doi.org/10.1080/19460171.2013.766024.

Sørensen, E., & Torfing, J. (2009). Making governance networks effective and democratic through metagovernance. *Public Administration, 87*(2), 234–258. https://doi.org/10.1111/j.1467-9299.2009.01753.x.

Spalla, F. (2005). L'analisi del decentramento urbano. In G. Fedel (Ed.), *Studi in Onore di Mario Stoppino* (pp. 131–140). Giuffrè: Milano.

Teles, F., & Swianiewicz, P. (2018). Motives for revisiting inter-municipal cooperation. In F. Teles (Ed.), *Inter-municipal cooperation in Europe* (pp. 1–13). Palgrave Macmillan.

Termeer, C. J. (2009). Barriers to new modes of horizontal governance: A sense-making perspective. *Public Management Review, 11*(3), 299–316. https://doi.org/10.1080/14719030902798180.

Torfing, J., Peters, B. G., Pierre, J., & Sørensen, E. (2012). *Interactive governance: Advancing the paradigm*. Oxford: Oxford university Press.

van Popering-Verkerk, J., & van Buuren, A. (2016). Decision-making patterns in multilevel governance: The contribution of informal and procedural interactions to significant multilevel decisions. *Public Management Review, 18*(7), 951–971. https://doi.org/10.1080/14719037.2015.1028974.

Vangen, S., Hayes, J. P., & Cornforth, C. (2015). Governing cross-sector, inter-organizational collaborations. *Public Management Review, 17*(9), 1237–1260. https://doi.org/10.1080/14719037.2015.1028974.

Verweij, S., Klijn, E. H., Edelenbos, J., & Van Buuren, A. (2013). What makes governance networks work? A fuzzy set qualitative comparative analysis of 14 Dutch spatial planning projects. *Public Administration, 91*(4), 1035–1055. https://doi.org/10.1111/padm.12007.

Zahariadis, N. (2016). Setting the agenda on agenda setting: Definitions, concepts and controversies. In N. Zahariadis (Ed.), *Handbook of public policy agenda setting* (pp. 1–24). Northampton: Edward Elgar Publishing.

Chapter 4
Redesigning Territorialisation to Improve Planning and Management Capabilities in Social Policy. Change or Business as Usual?

Abstract In this chapter the reform's attempt concerning the organization of the Local Area Plans in Lombardy will be presented. How does the regional decree 7631/2017 work? How is it structured? Which are the implications, the aims and the opportunities of this reform?

The chapter will present the way in which the Local Area Plans coped with the new regional legislative framework, how they have complied with it and how they have failed.

This analysis gives us a composite picture, which shows a large variance among Lombardy's territories that differ from making a great push towards innovation – both in governance and policy terms – to being substantially immobile and resistant to change. This immobilism can be connected to a series of variables like a persistent resistance to change from the public administration sector, difficulty in embracing innovative practices, structural limits in governance instruments dedicated to territorial coordination, stalemate among actors (joint decision trap) and a certain "parochial" approach in inter-municipal courses of action that consider routinized procedures as the best options from which it would be a mistake to move away (path dependence).

Keywords Territorialisation · Social policies · Management · Area local plan · Lombardy · Local governance

4.1 The Guidelines for Change

The Regional Decree No. 7631 was approved in December 2017 by the Lombardy regional government with the ambition of activating a process for redefining the Local Area Plans numbers and borders, by employing a partial top down strategy based on a mechanism of monetary reward, in order to conclude the rebuilding strategy of the governance model of the regional welfare system. The idea was to rationalise the extremely high number of Local Area Plans (98) and the governance of the territorial social assistance system by creating larger and better structured

© The Author(s), under exclusive license to Springer Nature Switzerland AG 2021
P. Previtali, E. Salvati, *Local Welfare and the Organization of Social Services*,
https://doi.org/10.1007/978-3-030-66128-1_4

Local Area Plans, able to define more effective models of inter-municipal cooperation. The task of enforcing these agreements, differently from some evidence provided by literature (Bel and Warner 2016), was not connected to cost saving needs
or the reduction of services, but had the aim of enforcing financial and service effectiveness by improving coordination, an approach that was thought could guarantee
longer term and more efficient agreements (Aldag and Warner 2018).

The General Director of the Department for Social Services of the Lombardy
Regional Government had this to say: this new regional strategy "(…) *is the product
of a broader reflection about the future of our regional welfare system. A reflection
brought about by the economic crisis and its effects and enforced by a renewed
consciousness about the role of municipalities in the definition of social policies. We
are aware of the need to have stronger Local Area Plans, more structured, able to
cope more easily with the new competencies and tasks that they have to fulfil. This
strategy mixes old elements – the confirmation of some macro goals like the enforcement of the integration degree between social and healthcare dimensions – and
innovative targets like the redefinition of the Local Area Plans borders plus a more
evident role for social innovation processes located at the local level*".

This new regional approach is unavoidably based on the assumption that the role
of the Local Area Plans has fundamentally changed over the last few years. Local
Area Plans have broadened in their scopes and functions, moving from the simple
role of "management" of basic social policies and the supplier (cash dispenser) of
national and regional monetary resources, to the role of planner and (partial) policy
maker with the responsibility of coordinating the various social actors that operate
in the social system's chain, as well as screening the efficiency and effectiveness of
social policies. This new role can be defined as the product of several structural
innovations:

- the evolution of citizens' needs and the presence of new social risks (traceable
  both in the social and healthcare fields),
- the transfer of resources and responsibilities to municipalities and Local Area
  Plans from superior levels of government (regional, national, European), from a
  perspective that is increasingly multilevel (Gualini 2006; Barberis et al. 2010),
- the changes produced by the reform of the Lombardy social-healthcare system.

As we saw in the first chapter, the Italian national framework over the years has
pushed increasingly to move the elaboration of the answer to social needs from the
national to local level in a perspective linked to the regionalisation of social provisions (Madama 2008; Kazepov and Barberis 2013). Unfortunately, the perspective
of integration set out by the national Law No. 328/2000, a model of local governance based on negotiation and participation, with an increasing convergence
among different regional arrangements (Battistella et al. 2004), has remained largely
unactuated during the last decade. The result is that nowadays the framework is
characterised by a substantial fragmentation of social policies, depending on the 20
Italian regions which can actuate completely autonomous choices in this field
(Kazepov and Barberis 2013). But a further element of fragmentation can be traced
back to the differentiation produced at the subnational level as a product of weak

regionalism, due to the fact that not all the Italian regions have the strength and the political authority to impose fully responsible political choices in a field like the one of social assistance, where the main competencies are in the hands of municipalities (Agostini 2008).

These contradictions are exacerbated in the RL where these shortcomings are side-lined by a high level of institutional fragmentation: a region with more than ten million inhabitants, with a population density of 421 inhabitants/km^2, divided into 1506 municipalities (with an average of 6.600 inhabitants per municipalities) with 98 Local Area Plans in charge of coordinating social policies. At the heart of the Regional action there is the ambition to reduce fragmentation with a partial top down strategy, without infringing on the autonomy of municipalities and Local Area Plans. From this point of view, the main goal is represented by the definition of a path able to strengthen coordination among municipalities, in order to better cope with the dilemmas at a territorial scale and service/resource fragmentation. A strengthening that is mainly rooted in the past experience of shared actions and cooperation in services provision, so to be "easily" improved on the "administrative memories" of previous established cooperation (Aldag and Warner 2018; Silva et al. 2018). From this point of view the legislative provision resulted ambitious because it implied both a high level of intensity in its scope (the final goal was the merger of Local Area Plans) and a highly variable level of inclusiveness[1] (the number of involved Local Area Plans) (Champion and Bonoli 2011).

In order to reach this goal the RL, for the first time in its legislative acts, has recognised the central role exerted by Local Area Plans in planning and providing social services, thus officially identifying the Local Area Plan as the main governance player for local welfare functioning. By means of this choice the Local Area Plans' planning role seems no longer to be considered as simply derived from a devolution of a function from the upper level of government, but as a proper and peculiar function of this arena, characterised by concrete autonomy in defining the strategic choices for their territories. This aspect is particularly evident if we take into consideration, for example, the new competencies given to the Local Area Plans by the RL in a delicate field like social housing.

From our interviews it has emerged that to reach this goal the main instrument employed by the Regional government is the support given to redefining the governance model in local welfare. In the words of the General Director *"a change able to strengthen the effectiveness (of local government) by reaching a new equilibrium in the model of welfare territorialisation. A step which became unavoidable after the approbation of the Law No. 23/2015 which has changed the governance system of the social-healthcare model and given birth to new regional agencies that operate in the territory"*.

In fact the Decree No. 7631 has as its primary goal the translation and application of the governance changes produced with the Law No. 23 in the social field, in

---

[1] This because the formation of the new Local Area Plans would not necessarily be the result of a fusion among just two Local Area Plan but could involve more territories.

particular for what concerns the delineation of a new "optimal level" useful for defining the administrative territorial borders for the supply of social services. The main criteria used to define the new borders of the Local Area Plans is connected to the number of inhabitants within the administrative borders: the Law No. 23/2015 and Decree No. 7631/2017 determined that no Local Area Plan can have less than 80.000 inhabitants (25.000 inhabitants for the mountain zones of Lombardy). At the time of the legislative provision, 48 out of 98 Local Area Plans did not respect this new threshold; a threshold that has the aim of definitively redefining the geography of social services in the region.

4.2   The Process of Change

In order to encourage territorial aggregations, the new guidelines are based on an innovative (at least for the RL) mechanism of award: the constitution of a new (district area, DA) will be rewarded with a sum of 30.000 euros. Interestingly, the regional government clearly indicated that the sum must be dedicated to the enforcement of the administrative structure of the Local Area Plans and their capability for action, thus confirming that the motivation behind the measure was the enforcement and institutionalisation of the new DA and not a mere numeric rationalisation. Furthermore, from this perspective, the decree explicitly required that the municipalities which make up the new Local Area Plan "must transfer congruous amounts of resources (monetary, employee and work space) to definitively strengthening the Local Area Plan and making it the nucleus for the planning of social policies at the territorial level". These new aggregations should not be the product of a simple sum of municipalities, but should be the result of an aggregation of actors who have previously operated in strict coordination and that are now able to promote a brand new planning model for social policies in an enlarged territory. This course of action confirms that the RL's target was the creation of stable and long term structured inter-municipal agreements (Bel and Warner 2016; Silva et al. 2018).

The access to the grant was articulated in different chronological steps (Table 4.1) in order to give the opportunity to all the territories to structure the aggregation path according to their own needs, peculiarities and time necessities. The sum was higher for those who presented the new Local Area Plan in the first step because it means that they had constructed their planning phase in a shorter time and were still operating while having a different scale and model of governance as their reference point.

Table 4.1 Steps for the access to the regional contribution

	First step, before June 30, 2018	Second step, between the first of July and December 31, 2018	Third step, between the first of January 2019 and December 312,019
Amount gained by the local area plan	€ 30.000,00	€ 20.000,00	€ 10.000,00

The definition of the new Local Area Plan and of a new model of governance, then gave the opportunity to access a second level of contribution which was strictly connected to policy making goals and a social innovation approach. The regional government defined three policy areas in which the Local Area Plans had the opportunity to plan and realise new policies. These areas were identified as "strategical" because they concerned policy fields considered as particularly important for the planning of social services and because they could provide a substantial boost to the enforcement of the Local Area Plans' policy making capacity. The three areas concerned:

1. projects aimed at defining the requirements for citizens' access to and participation in services and interventions, through tools such as: uniformity of regulations, access criteria, ISEE thresholds,[2] the family factor, etc.;
2. projects aimed at defining common requirements, parameters and indicators for the evaluation of the quality and appropriateness of structures and services, through tools, also experimental, that lead to the homogeneity of evaluation criteria (e.g. shared calls for proposals, result indicators, etc.);
3. planning dedicated to social innovation (new services, innovative ways of responding to new needs, innovative paths of care, etc.) thanks to co-planning/ co-realisation of services through partnerships with the Third Sector.

These three areas were mainly conceived for the new Local Area Plan that would come into existence after the application of the reform, but it is the first area that is particularly suited to a new Local Area Plan because its aim is to guarantee territorial homogeneity in the access to social services in a brand new aggregation (that can be considered as heterogeneous in its new arrangements both in terms of services and access criteria). As outlined in our interviews the two reward levels are conceived as strictly connected because: *"(...) a new governance model, with larger Local Area Plans (in terms of inhabitants) and a more efficient administrative structure, is fundamental to planning in a more effective way and is the prerequisite to introducing real innovative elements in the actions promoted at the local level"*.

These double but interconnected channels of action respond to a need for the public actor to stimulate a difficult administrative reform in the governance of local welfare more effectively (Champion and Bonoli 2011): a change that, in the mind of the RL's government, should be approached with a view to providing a more innovative and efficient idea of social services. A nested structure more capable of introducing new instruments useful for providing innovative answers to new social needs. By means of Decree No. 7631, the RL also codified the role of its territorial agencies in the governance of social services supply, by giving the ATS the function of: (a) supporting Local Area Plans in their planning and supply functions, and, (b) improving the level of integration between the social and healthcare systems.

---

[2] The ISEE is a mathematical instrument used to measure the overall economic level of the household, considering - with some exceptions - all the items of "wealth" attributable to that same household, such as real estate, financial annuities, miscellaneous income, etc.

This legislative choice means that the ATS has the responsibility of actively contributing to the reduction of fragmentation in the chain of welfare supply – considering both social and healthcare policies – and of actively coordinating the different actors operating in the system. The RL created the ATS with the goal of having an actor better able to institutionalise the relationships between the territorial actors, to coordinate their actions and to provide a useful – in the words of our interviewee *"institutional instrument able to enforce the governance of local welfare, while reducing the costs of coordination between actors and the dispersion of resources, knowledge and experiences"*. Summing up this aspect with the redrawing of the Local Area Plans borders, highlights the ambition of the regional government to follow up on redefining the regional welfare territorialisation model.

Furthermore, the new strategic lines for the Local Area Plans have the ambition to better institutionalise the role of the Third Sector within the planning and supply phases, thus recognising the Local Area Plan as the "arena of governance" within which the cooperation and coordination between the various actors of the network must take place. For this reason the regional decree requests that the new Local Area Plans institutionalise the presence of technical-political tables for the combined work between municipalities and social actors, in order to promote a more innovative model of response to social needs.

The elements that make these guidelines for the model of social services' territorialisation in the RL strategic and innovative are:

- the focus on the administrative and governance strengthening of the ATS as the arena in which social services and local welfare can be planned and realised;
- enforcing the process of changing the Local Area Plans as a means to reducing the high level of resource dispersion;
- the strengthening of the "network" by the redefinition of borders: an equilibrium between the Local Area Plans' dimension and its closeness to citizens' needs;
- the idea that a bigger and better organised Local Area Plan means a greater ability to manage broader policies like social housing, the fight against poverty and social exclusion;
- the definition of a new role for Local Area Plans in the implementation phase of social – healthcare integration;
- improving the Local Area Plans' ability to coordinate the different actions/resources which are defined/supplied at different levels of government;
- the opportunity for the Local Area Plans to improve their policy making ability;
- the opportunity to reconsider the administrative structure of the Local Area Plans.

The Lombardy model even after the reform produced by the Law No. 23/2015, needs to (try to) "contain" the predominance of the healthcare sector, which is a peculiarity of a regional welfare model unbalanced in favour of hospitals and healthcare supply to the detriment of the social sector (Agostini 2008; Gori 2018).

The new strategic lines – along with the previous ones for the years 2015–2017 – represent both a systematic attempt to promote the centrality of the Local Area Plans as the instrument for the strengthening of social planning, and an attempt to stimulate a revision of the Local Area Plans' borders and governance in order to "promote a virtuous mechanism of empowerment" for these actors. From this point of view this strategy represents a partial break away from the regional implementation strategy that in the last 20 years was characterised by a strictly top-down model, with highly centralised policy decisions and a low level of territorial autonomy (Lumino and Pirone 2013).

As we have previously underlined, the decree clearly required municipalities to commit to enforcing the Local Area Plans in terms of resources and staff in order to strengthen the efficiency of this instrument that can be organised and managed freely by the municipalities that make it up. This is particularly important because in Italy the majority of the monetary resources dedicated to social policies derive from the budget of municipalities which, alongside the transfer of resources from the central government and the Region, have the opportunity to only partially shape the budget for social policies and, consequently, the aims to pursue (except for some mandatory actions connected to well defined categories of users like disabled people). In a national framework characterised by a high level of intra-national and intra-regional fragmentation, with a high number of municipalities (Ranci and Popolizio 2013), the enforcement of the Local Area Plans and their rationalisation (both in terms of borders and total number) means operating to reduce the level of variability in an effort of institutional recomposition and to define a better "governance of the governance" (Previtali and Salvati 2019).

The renewed role and centrality of the Local Area Plans as outlined by Decree No. 7631, represents the attempt to find a new equilibrium between the desire to improve proximity between citizens and services, and the need to have governance actors strong enough to plan and provide new and innovative services, which are able to cope with the new social needs. Only new, "larger and better structured and equipped Local Area Plans" (Interviews) can embody the new centrality of the public actor within the network of social services in the region, where the role of the local institutions is to act as the network orchestrator and the glue of a fragmented system.

4.3   From Where We Were Taking Off

Two supporting elements have driven the legislator in the definition of the new guidelines for the planning of social services of the Lombardy Local Area Plans: governance and planning. The former is the "context" in which these new guidelines have been conceived, that is the already mentioned Law No. 23/2015 reform of the social-healthcare system, which sought to revise the regional welfare system. The reform, although particularly focused on the health and socio-healthcare dimensions, foresees a revolution in the system of the territorial governance of services that substantially affects and influences also the organisation of the social sector.

The old Local Healthcare Authorities and Hospitals have been replaced by two new agencies following a purely functional logic: the new ASSTs provide regional healthcare and social-healthcare services, while the ATSs have the governance of the entire system and, above all, must work to strengthen the integration between the healthcare and social dimensions. The ATS therefore have a fundamental task, as a regional agency on the territory, of coordinating the territorial actors and their policy efforts (planning and delivery). The previous guidelines for zonal planning for the 3-year period 2015–2017 aimed at understanding how to build innovative responses to the new social needs that have emerged in recent years, by strengthening the network of local welfare services (Salvati 2016). The main issue identified by the legislator in order to improve this response was that of integration, i.e. the effort to overcome the sub-regional fragmentation that characterises the system. To this end, the guidelines identified three areas in which to make an effort: the managing of resources, knowledge/information and services.

The two pillars on which the new programming guidelines were based highlight two elements which at first glance may seem divergent: a state of fragmentation of the social system (in terms of organisation, governance, services, etc.) and the strategic need to strengthen the territorial dimension of social services planning/provision and build more efficient services closer to the needs of citizens.

Such ambitious goals have nevertheless taken into account a regional context that is very complex, with structured caveats connected to the fact that in Lombardy a high level of institutional fragmentation persists. We are talking of a region with more than ten million inhabitants who are divided into 1506 municipalities (1034 municipalities have less than 5000 inhabitants) and with 98 Area Social Plans in charge of planning and coordinating social services.

The problematic issue that the regional policy maker has decided to address is that of rethinking the model of governance and action of the Plans through a review of the organisational model (Salvati 2016), in order to enhance their effectiveness and reinforce the flexibility of the Local Area Plan in designing and implementing policies, since proximity to the citizen cannot in itself be considered sufficient to guaranteeing effective services. Services which, in view of the evolution of the Lombardy welfare model envisage the centrality of new principles such as personalisation, timeliness, temporariness and co-responsibility, as methods of intervention which should characterise the social field. These principles, linked to the new organisation produced by Decree No. 7631/2017 embody the turning point that the RL has also outlined for the Local Area Plans.

4.4   Regional Decree No. 7631/2017: A Change of Pace for Zonal Planning

Decree no. 7631 had to deal with the issue of the new planning phase in a substantially evolving context for the regional welfare system, which was going through significant changes determined by both structural/governance elements (the reform of the governance of the social-health system) and policy factors – the new approach to social policies, in particular on the issue of social inclusion and innovation, considered as drivers for social change (Cajaiba-Santana 2014) – as well as problems related to the emergence of new needs and the planning of new responses (although this is a long-term issue, which can be traced back to the outbreak of the economic crisis in 2008).

The starting point for this guideline is the confirmation of what Decree No. 2941/2014 provided for in the 2015–2017 planning phase, that is the focus on "recomposing", i.e. the need to continue towards a reduction in fragmentation as regards information (knowledge), services and resources. From this point of view, the previous 3-year period remains in the background as a reference framework. In this framework, it is the *Ufficio di Piano* that takes on a paramount strategic importance for the design of territorial policy making. The DGR does not assign new functions – it is not its task or duty – but recognises for the first time, by making a strong political-administrative act, the strategic role of the Local Area Plan as a global player in social policies. If in the first part of their existence the *Ufficio di Piano* were mainly focused on the management/distribution function of monetary resources (through vouchers, bonus etc.) and basic social services, this role has evolved over the course of time and has determined a substantial change in the mission of the Local Area Plan. This is due to the fact that at the Local Area Plan level there is an increasing concentration of functions and tasks: management, planning, needs analysis and delivery of local services and of some regional measures. This means that the *Ufficio di Piano* is responsible for managing a number of functions and activities that until a few years ago were not foreseeable. According to the regional legislator, the Decree acknowledges this change and begins to take on the need to support this changed role. In particular because it is evident that at the moment the Local Area Plan is responsible for the task of territorially coordinating and integrating (when possible) the social interventions and measures produced at national and regional levels, with specific interventions autonomously designed by the Local Area Plans. In a nutshell: it is the sub regional level that has to recompose the fragmentation produced at national and regional levels. The purpose of the regional decree is therefore not only to recognise a planning capacity derived (from other levels), but also to support a direct territorial planning capacity, which can be enhanced by the ability to integrate the reading of needs and the autonomous design of local policies, with regional and national measures. This ideational feature is particularly evident in the second part of the decree, dedicated to social innovation.

As we have previously seen, the guidelines can be divided into two main strands: the first concerns the revision of territorial governance and the role of the Local Area Plan, the second is dedicated to supporting the definition of new policies dedicated to service quality, equal access to services for citizens and innovation. In both areas there is a significant novelty represented by the introduction of a reward mechanism in order to encourage and support the Local Area Plans.

The reward model highlights the regional government's willingness to support the Local Area Plan in a process of rationalisation and recognise their planning function, but at the same time it does not ignore the fact that Local Area Plans are free to act in different ways and, consequently, distinctions among them should be made with respect to their capacity to implement the guidelines.

4.4.1   First Step: Reach the Optimal Size for the New District Area

The main point around which the reflection on the revision of the governance model and the implementation of the principle of services – citizens' proximity revolves, is that fragmentation does not mean efficient and effective territorialisation.

Table 4.2 shows us the state of the Lombardy Local Area Plans on the eve of the launch of Decree No.7631/2017. The picture that emerges quite clearly is the high level of fragmentation in the Lombardy governance structure with 98 Local Area Plans that each cover an average population of 88,000 inhabitants. In reality, the average figure is obviously misleading and to understand the real fragmentation and territorial dispersion, it is necessary to look at Table 4.3, where the numbers of all the Lombardy Local Area Plans, grouped by reference ATS, are reported in detail. Within each single ATS it is possible to identify Plans with very different numbers in terms of population, demonstrating that there is great variety and dissimilarity in the structure of territorial governance.

The level of fragmentation in the territorial organisation of social services therefore appears incontrovertible. Except for the ATS della Montagna that accounts for an entire mountain territory and the two ATS of Città Metropolitana di Milano and Brianza which cover an area of high population density, the other territories are quite similar, and show a level of dissimilarity that is difficult to explain if not in terms of "parochialism" and a lack of propensity to establish larger inter-municipal forms of coordination.

Table 4.2 Local Area Plans in the RL at 31-12-2017 (divided according to the corresponding ATS)

ATS	No.- of social-healthcare districts (ASST)	No. of Local Area Plans (LR 3/2008)	Average population for Local Area Plans
CITTA' METROPOLITANA DI MILANO	6 (9 ASST)	19	116.226 (not considering the city of Milan)
INSUBRIA	3	19	75.362
MONTAGNA	2	8	41.936
BRIANZA	3	8	150.666
BERGAMO	3	14	79.164
BRESCIA	3	12	96.951
VALPADANA	3	9	85.924
PAVIA	1	9	60.881
REGIONE LOMBARDIA	24 (27 ASST)	98	88.389

Table 4.3 The Local Area Plans in Lombardy at 31/12/2017

ATS	PIANO DI ZONA (LR 3/2008)	No. of member municipalities	TOT Population
Città metropolitana di Milano	Milano Città	1	1.345.851
	Cernusco Sul Naviglio	9	119.709
	Melzo	8	83.810
	Pioltello	4	93.623
	Trezzo D'Adda	7	42.254
	Binasco	7	51.252
	Rozzano	4	74.042
	Paullo	5	56.646
	San Giuliano Milanese	9	111.200
	Corsico	6	119.619
	Garbagnate Milanese	8	192.304
	Rho	9	171.509
	Castano Primo	11	70.239
	Legnano	11	188.837
	Abbiategrasso	15	82.174
	Magenta	13	128.173
	Cinisello Balsamo	4	140.345
	Sesto San Giovanni	2	129.579
	Casalpusterlengo – Lodi – Sant'Angelo Lodigiano	62	236.756
	TOT Local Area Plan 19	**133**	**3.201.166**
Ats dell'Insubria	Campione d'Italia	1	1.995
	Cantù	9	76.133
	Mariano Comense	6	57.990
	Como	23	140.445
	Erba	25	71.285
	Lomazzo – Fino Mornasco	19	103.328
	Olgiate Comasco	21	90.613
	Arcisate	11	49.974
	Laveno	26	71.408
	Luino	24	56.019
	Azzate	13	52.099
	Sesto Calende	13	50.518
	Tradate	8	55.835
	Varese	12	114.362
	Busto Arsizio	1	83.106
	Castellanza	7	65.803
	Gallarate	9	123.661
	Saronno	6	96.452
	Somma Lombardo	9	70.853
	TOT Local Area Plan 19	**243**	**1.431.879**

(continued)

Table 4.3 (continued)

ATS	PIANO DI ZONA (LR 3/2008)	No. of member municipalities	TOT Population
Ats della Montagna	Bormio	6	24.965
	Chiavenna	12	24.816
	Morbegno	25	47.036
	Sondrio	22	56.273
	Tirano	12	28.622
	Dongo	16	17.427
	Menaggio	31	36.027
	Valcamonica	41	100.323
	TOT Local Area Plan 8	**165**	**335.489**
Ats della Brianza	Bellano	32	53.366
	Lecco	32	165.864
	Merate	24	120.024
	Desio	7	192.503
	Monza	3	170.820
	Carate Brianza	13	152.691
	Seregno	10	168.177
	Vimercate	22	181.885
	TOT Local Area Plan 8	**143**	**1.205.330**
Ats di Bergamo	Bergamo	6	152.373
	Valle Brembana	37	42.136
	Valle Imagna e Villa d'Almè	20	52.839
	Dalmine	17	145.519
	Isola Bergamasca	24	133.309
	Romano di Lombardia	17	84.602
	Treviglio	18	111.127
	Alto Sebino	10	30.952
	Monte Bronzone – Basso Sebino	12	31.889
	Valle Cavallina	20	54.444
	Albino (Valle Seriana)	18	98.739
	Valle Seriana Superiore e Valle di Scalve	24	43.221
	Grumello	8	49.676
	Seriate	11	77.472
	TOT Local Area Plan 14	**242**	**1.108.298**

(continued)

Table 4.3 (continued)

ATS	PIANO DI ZONA (LR 3/2008)	No. of member municipalities	TOT Population
Ats di Brescia	Brescia	2	201.102
	Brescia Ovest	11	101.002
	Brescia Est	13	97.702
	Valle Trompia	18	112.294
	Sebino	12	55.139
	Monte Orfano	6	59.852
	Oglio Ovest	11	95.388
	Bassa Bresciana Occidentale	15	57.191
	Bassa Bresciana Centrale	20	116.572
	Bassa Bresciana Orientale	7	66.643
	Garda – Salò	22	125.135
	Valle Sabbia	27	75.387
	TOT Local Area Plan 12	**164**	**1.163.407**
Ats della Valpadana	Mantova	15	156.317
	Asola	12	45.988
	Guidizzolo	9	64.912
	Ostiglia	17	44.750
	Suzzara	6	52.981
	Viadana	10	47.920
	Casalmaggiore	20	39.199
	Cremona	47	158.022
	Crema	48	163.223
	TOT Local Area Plan 9	**184**	**773.312**
Ats di Pavia	Garlasco	27	55.100
	Mortara	20	42.108
	Vigevano	4	83.150
	Broni	26	40.297
	Casteggio	28	34.375
	Voghera	23	66.552
	Certosa	24	75.806
	Corteolona	25	45.388
	Pavia	12	105.150
	TOT Local Area Plan 9	**189**	**547.926**

With regards to this aspect, the first normative intervention is represented by the Law No. 23/2015 that in Article No. 7bis states that: *"(...) Districts are divided by the ATS into district areas, each comprising a population normally not less than 80,000 inhabitants. In areas with high population density this ratio increases up to 120,000 inhabitants. In mountain areas and areas with a low population density, the area may comprise a minimum population of 25,000 inhabitants. For the Metropolitan City of Milan, the districts and the relative articulation in district areas take into account the functional territorial articulation of the same"*.

The new guidelines are therefore based on the implementation of a regulatory framework which, although it is driven by the centrality of the healthcare sector, has expressed the need to move towards a reduction in the organisational fragmentation (Previtali and Salvati 2019), with an effort towards enforced territorialisation that takes into account the need to pursue new and better scales for social services (Aldag and Warner 2018). The decree then outlines the functional transition from the old Local Area Plan to the new and enlarged Local Area Plan, a necessary element to define the governance structures that rule the system. However, this aggregation effort does not just respond to a mere criterion of numerical rationalisation based on the population, but also seeks to encourage the implementation and institutionalisation of cooperation and shared work that – during the previous 20 years – have brought together many Local Area Plans. In fact, the decree states quite explicitly that the aim is to: *"(...) strengthen supra-zonal cooperation relations that in the course of the years and of the previous three year periods have been formed, with the aim of strengthening and homogenising fundamental aspects of services in territories that have similar socio/economic characteristics and are contiguous in terms of territorial/administrative borders. This means thinking of horizontal cooperation as a model of governance to be further strengthened by mobilising resources that encourage the structuring of such relations"*.

At the heart of this approach there is the idea that the revision of the Local Area Plans' boundaries so as to constitute the new *district areas*, should not be interpreted as a mere compliance with the disposition of a law – a clear limitation of many acts transposed by the Italian Public Administration – but as a window of opportunity useful for strengthening the increasingly important role of the Local Area Plan as a hub of social policies at the local level (Salvati 2016). Considering that the overall picture is in a phase of constant evolution, these guidelines, in accordance with the intent of the regional government, respond to a logic that sees the structural setting of the Local Area Plan within the framework defined by Law No. 23/2015, which preserves the autonomy of municipalities and maintains the Region's role in the field of social welfare policies.

From this point of view the push towards territorial reorganisation and the new features in the governance of services produced by Law No. 23 are obviously not unrelated, mainly due to the creation of the ATS and ASST. In particular, it is the role of the ATS that intersects with the dynamics of the functioning of the Local Area Plan, this because, in the background, there is always the long-standing question of integration between the social and healthcare dimensions (Agostini 2008).

In order to realise this territorial integration, the reform identifies the ATS as the structure responsible for the governance of this process because they have the innovative task of governing the territorial network of services, and promoting coordination actions between actors and on the actions undertaken. If it is true that the social functions are exclusively in the hands of the municipalities, it is also true that the creation of a territorial agency dedicated to the overall governance of the network and to the integration function between the social and health dimensions, pinpoints the willingness to strengthen the territorial dimension of welfare, supporting it through its dedicated territorial structures in order to reduce the costs of coordination, the planning function of municipalities and the Local Area Plan.

In short, the network is more structured with the presence of an institutional player that, as Previtali and Salvati (2019) write, has the task of creating the conditions to support the integration of services directly on the territory, with a logic that favours greater horizontality, also in terms of subsidiarity. A horizontality that sees, however, a new role for the public actor, unlike what happened in previous periods, much more oriented exclusively to the logic of the construction of the quasi-market and the principle of vertical subsidiarity.

In this framework the mechanism of reward is the incentive to push the Local Area Plan to review their boundaries in order to move towards a better and optimal territorial dimension for the *area district*. This concept could be defined as follows: "the definition of a new territorial space that enables an excess of fragmentation and particularism in the governance of services to be overcome by reducing the costs of coordination, and which at the same time is able to exploit already developed territorial paths of cooperation and coordination, allowing a strengthening of the territorial governance model and a better use of resources (human, economic and instrumental)". A fragmentation whose containment was not facilitated by the coexistence of the health and social-healthcare districts. The Healthcare District can be defined as an organisational-functional articulation of the former ASL, which has the task of improving the level of integration between the different services concerning health and social welfare services, so as to allow a coordinated and continuous response to the health needs of the population. The District should have the responsibility of governing the demand (assessing which services and for which needs) and ensuring the management of territorial health services (with a production/providing role), although the national legislation has not specified the forms and modalities of this competence. In Lombardy, the Social district (the Local Area Plan) and Healthcare District organise unified access to take care of social and health needs through the Single Access Point. This territorial reception point, is able to provide information, activate questions and practices, submit requests for assistance involving the expertise of several structures, and receive complaints. So for Lombardy the paramount problem is that, unlike what happens in many Italian regions such as Emilia-Romagna, Friuli Venezia Giulia, Marche, Molise, Val d'Aosta and Veneto, where the healthcare district coincides with the social district, there is no coincidence (total or almost) or overlapping between the territorial governance of the social and healthcare systems. An organisational obstacle that undermines the possibility of having a unitary and effectively integrated planning dimension: a handicap also exacerbated by the high number of territorial areas (Table 4.3) among which the governance of the social system is fragmented and that requests a supplementary effort in order to improve coordination.

Decree No. 7631 determines that the assignment of the first tranche of the monetary award is dedicated to the development of the new zonal aggregation and the creation of the new *area district*. This means that the municipalities that maintain the current subdivision into territorial areas in accordance with the former Law No. 3/2008 will not be eligible for the bonus, unless they already comply with the inhabitants' parameters determined by Article 7 *bis* of Law No. 23. In practice, Local Area Plans that are already of an optimal size/dimension can still qualify for the award. The sense of this choice is to be found in the fact that this bonus is aimed at developing and consolidating the planning capacity of the Local Area Plan, and for this reason the Regional government did not want to preclude those who already have the optimal dimension from building the new planning also in virtue of these new objectives and guidelines. Access to the bonus is divided into several windows, in order to give the territories the opportunity to structure their own route according to their peculiar needs, except that the award for those who decide to immediately activate the new dimension is higher, since it means setting the new 3-year planning by virtue of a governance already modified and built on the new boundaries. Although the contribution may appear small in its amount (30,000 euros), the important element from a policy making point of view is the use, for the first time in a systemic way, of an incentive mechanism aimed at improving the strength of the Local Area Plans as territorial policy makers. This approach has as its ideational basis, the awareness that from the reorganisation of the Local Area Plans and their subsequently more efficient functioning, stems the capacity of the local welfare system to respond to the new and multiple challenges.

Sadly, the final results of this reforming effort have been quite disappointing, due to the low number of Local Area Plans that have accepted the Regional input to redefine their borders and their organisational arrangements. At the end of 2020 (Table 4.6) there are 7 new Local Area Plans that are the result of a fusion between 14 of the previously existing Local Area Plans. The total number of documents for social planning which have been signed and sent to Lombardy government are 70. This means that another 21 Local Area Plans are missing and that they have decided not to define a new plan for social services in the 2018–2020 triennium, but instead to apply a deferment/prorogation of the 2015–2017 social planning, without upgrading the social planning according to new needs, data and services.

As outlined in Table 4.4, the few Local Area Plans that decided to create a new *district area*, were scattered between the three timing windows defined by the regional government. Just one Local Area Plan in all the Region – the Local Area Plan of Lomellina – was established in the first step, so gaining the entire award provided by the decree. Except for the new Local Area Plan Visconteo Sud, all the others aggregations were defined in the final weeks before the deadline for the decree's reward mechanism: this suggests that even the Local Area Plans that successfully reached the goal, had some serious difficulties and troubles in constructing the new *district area*. Despite the fact that during some interviews carried out before the definition of the new guidelines, representatives of both the ATS and the Local Area Plans had recognised – among others themes – the limits in the action capacity of the *district area*, the need to pursue "scale policies" and the existence of rooted collaboration with neighbourhood Local Area Plans, the various territories were found unprepared for such radical change.

Let's now turn to one of the questions which this book wants to address. What are the main obstacles that have hindered the success of the reform provided for by the decree? The first is the willingness of the territories to take on and set up the new territorial reorganisation. From some interviews carried out with the political and technical actors of municipalities and Local Area Plans, it has emerged that the creation of a new Local Area Plan was not considered desirable for some very simple reasons: (1) the fear of losing control over social policies by becoming part of a

Table 4.4 New Local Area Plans in Lombardy as of 30/01/2020

ATS	Local Area Plan	Result of the fusion (if it is a new Local Area Plan)	Timing
Città Metropolitana di Milano	Alto Milanese	Castano	31/12/2019
		Legnano	
	Visconteo Sud Milano	Rozzano	31/12/2018
		Pieve Emanuele	
Val Padana	Oglio Po	Casalasco	31/12/2019
		Viadanese	
Pavia	Alto e Basso Pavese	Certosa	31/12/2019
		Corteolona	
	Broni e Casteggio	Broni and Casteggio	31/12/2019
	Lomellina	Garlasco	30/06/2018
		Mortara	
		Vigevano	
	Voghera	Voghera and Mountain community (previously it was within the former Casteggio Local Area Plan)	31/12/2018

wider aggregation; (2) the fear of affecting consolidated organisational routines; (3) the fear of the representatives of Local Area Plans made up of small and medium-sized municipalities of associating with Local Area Plans with large municipalities (we can call it the "dominion risk"); and, (4) a certain "municipal parochialism" that seeks to preserve the municipality as (or inter-municipal aggregation) autonomous and fully recognisable; a condition that makes relationships with other municipalities of the territory difficult at times. The latter can be defined as "political resistance", which denotes the absence of a political leadership able to cope with new challenges and that operates as a barrier to change. The second element of concern is the capacity to plan and equip a new Local Area Plan with the governance tools appropriate for facing the new challenges, both of an organisational and policy making nature. The network model, with its system of pooled resources and the institutionalisation of new relationships of trust and coordination, can be considered as an interesting outlet for solving problems of coordination, trust and collective action but requires the political/organisational will, technical/administrative capacities and the abilities to plan new management arrangements of people and resources, three elements that are not always easy to find (contextually) in the local political/administrative context. The third critical aspect is the availability of resources for the implementation of such a significant change. If it is true that the decree introduces an economic reward, although small, it is not clear at the moment whether the regional government intends to deploy other resources to support the new Local Area Plans that could arise from the aggregations. The final element for concern is uncertainty about the future, something which weighs heavily on the choices that the actors are willing to make. So, a mix of political and technical resistances, the difficulty of losing routinized organisational models and designing new arrangements, the lack of resources and a high level of uncertainty have all created an explosive mix which validly explains the substantial failure of the regional government provision.

A failure that seems to have missed the opportunity of reaching an increased and better performing coordination, as well as a reduction in fragmentation by applying an advanced inter-municipal cooperation model. A model that should represent progress compared to the simple associated management of functions, a model able to look beyond the narrower territorial context in order to better cope with the new social demands and the unanswered social needs (Silva et al. 2018; Saruis et al. 2019; Salvati 2020).

4.4.2   Second Step: Strategic Goals and Social Planning. A Matter of Compliance or a Boost for Innovation? A Quantitative Point of View

The second level of award shifts the focus of the Region's indications from the dimension of governance to that of policy making. The two areas, as seen above, are not alternative and distant, as stated by those who designed the decree, the sense is to reform the administrative space of governance in order to produce more effective policies, capable of responding to new needs and social risks (Salvati 2020).

At the basis of this approach there is the recognition that a local welfare system that is not effectively organised, has more problems in carrying out activities such as: the analysis of social needs and risks, the emergence of particularly critical and not immediately visible situations of social exclusion, the definition of a planning based on these needs and finally an optimal use of (scarce) resources.

This double channel of intervention aims to create a combination able to supply the public actor with the right tools with which to provide articulated and flexible responses to complex (more or less expressed) social needs, through the integration of available resources from different sources of funding and by enhancing the role of the various social actors and strengthening the structuring of governance arenas in a logic of increasing cooperation between the public and private realms (Da Roit and Sabatinelli 2005).

The indications provided by the regional government – as seen before –defined three macro areas on which the Local Area Plans have to work:

1. the definition of common requirements for citizens' access to and participation in services and interventions;
2. the definition of common requirements, parameters and indicators for the evaluation of the quality and appropriateness of structures and services;
3. the definition of policies/actions focused on social innovation through partnership with the Third Sector.

With the Decree No. 810 emanated in January 2019, the regional government defined a series of parameters/indicators useful for fulfilling the indicated policy tasks and evaluating the effectiveness and the feasibility of the proposed projects. The RL established a joint commission (composed of members of the regional staff, representatives from the ATS and university researchers) for the screening and approbation of the proposed projects. The work of the commission was to individuate those projects that were in compliance with the general and specific indications and that were eligible to be funded. The picture drawn of this second step of the Decree No. 7631 is quite composed and in the next section we will try to highlight the main evidence.

Overall, out of 71 *Local Area Plans* established by 31 December 2019, 54 (76%, Fig. 4.1) have submitted one or more projects to have access to the second award of the decree, this means that three-quarters of the *Ambiti* that have the requisites to participate in the selection process, effectively submitted policy projects. At the moment it is not possible to explain why 13 *Ambiti* did not present any project proposal even though they were eligible to.[3]

Considering that each Local Area Plan had the possibility to present up to 3 projects, one for each type of objective indicated by the decree, the total number of projects that could have been presented by the 54 Local Area Plans amounts to 162. The total number of projects actually submitted is 147 (91%, Fig. 4.2). This means that the response to the regional government policy making indications has been quite good, especially if compared to the Local Area Plan reactions to the first step of the decree. If we take a look at the submitted projects, we can appreciate that there is a fairly uniform distribution among the three types (Fig. 4.3): type one 34%, type two 33% and type three 33%.

As far as Objective 1 is concerned, an interesting preliminary reflection can be made. The aim of this objective was mainly to support the new *Local Area Plans*, on a path towards the homogenisation of access criteria and requirements, in order to assure an equal treatment to citizens and the effective supply of a social service tailored to the individual economic capabilities and social needs. A fundamental but at the same time complex goal, in the moment in which the fusion between two or more Local Area Plans is carried out. The total number of Local Area Plans that have submitted a proposal for this objective amounts to 50, but only 6 of them are the new *ones* born from a merger. This means that as many as 44 Local Area Plans structurally organised by almost 20 years of cooperation and associated management have not been able, during these two decades, to achieve an effective and full homogenisation of these criteria. This shows a significant delay and real disparity as regards the access of citizens to services/performance, and highlights how the effectiveness of social planning in previous years had not been reached, instead revealing a lack of homogeneity within well-established inter-municipal cooperation agreements and a concrete fragmentation in service access/delivery at the sub regional level.

---

[3] 4 Local Area Plans do not have the authorisation to access the second step because they planned the new Local Area Plan for the 2018–2020 period, even if they did not comply with the population parameters stated in the Decree No. 7631.

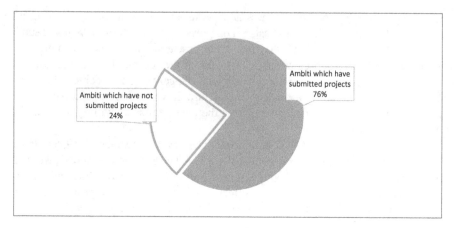

Fig. 4.1 Percentage of Local Area Plan which have submitted at least one project proposal

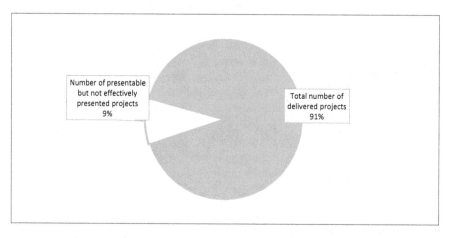

Fig. 4.2 Total amount of submitted projects compared to presentable but not effectively presented projects

Looking at the final outcome of the evaluation, it can be seen that a total of 88 projects out of 147 submitted (60%, Fig. 4.4) were approved by the regional commission and will therefore be funded. This data allows for a comment on the capacity of the Local Area Plans to devise projects: 40% of the projects were not approved because they did not comply with the evaluation requirements that were used for the selection. Considering that it was possible to use integration to overcome possible formal errors and/or lack of clarity in some steps of the design, this data underlines a shortcoming in the planning capacity of well-established Local Area Plans. This is particularly worrying as they often indicate in their planning documents that one of their objectives is to gain external funding through participation in competitive calls for proposals.

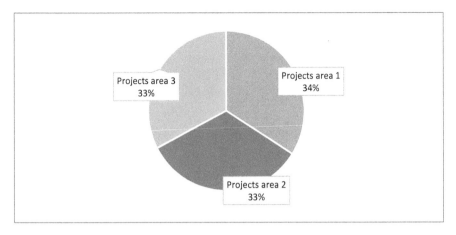

Fig. 4.3 Type of projects according to the strategic areas

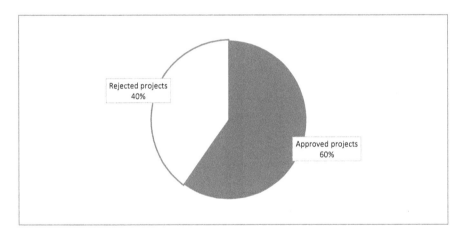

Fig. 4.4 Approved and rejected projects

By disaggregating the data according to the territorially competent ATS, we can proceed to compare these results and to get a picture of the distribution with respect to different areas of Lombardy. By analysing the number of Local Area Plans in each ATS that have submitted projects to access the second award tranche, we get an interesting snapshot of the actual situation, that is summarised in Table 4.5. In particular, all the Local Area Plans of ATS Valpadana and Brianza have submitted projects, the Local Area Plans of ATS Bergamo, Milan, Pavia and Montagna have submitted projects in at least 75% of the cases, while only half of the Local Area Plans of ATS Brescia and Insubria have presented projects.

Analysing the number of projects submitted and disaggregating the data by ATS we obtain the results summarised in Table 4.6. The Local Area Plans of the ATS Bergamo and Brianza that submitted projects did so for all three strategic objec-

Table 4.5 Total number of *Local Area Plans* by ATS

	Local area plans which have submitted projects	Local area plans which have not submitted projects	Local area plans at 31-12-2019
ATS BERGAMO	12	1	13
ATS BRESCIA	5	7	12
ATS BRIANZA	8	0	8
ATS INSUBRIA	6	5	11
ATS MILANO	9	1	10
ATS MONTAGNA	6	2	8
ATS PAVIA	4	1	5
ATS VALPADANA	4	0	4
	54	**17**	**71**

Table 4.6 Projects distribution according to ATS

	Total number of submitted projects	Number of presentable but not effectively presented projects	Total number of presentable projects
ATS BERGAMO	36	0	36
ATS BRESCIA	11	4	15
ATS BRIANZA	24	0	24
ATS INSUBRIA	15	3	18
ATS MILANO	25	2	27
ATS MONTAGNA	15	3	18
ATS PAVIA	11	1	12
ATS VALPADANA	10	2	12
	147	**15**	**162**

tives, while the Local Area Plans of the other ATS did so for at least two out of three objectives (at least 70% of the eligible projects). On the whole, therefore, it emerges that the *Local Area Plans* that participated did so by presenting projects that tried to respond as much as possible to the strategic objectives set out by the Region.

This is also confirmed by analysing in detail the type of projects, i.e. which strategic objective each of them responded to (Fig. 4.5). The distribution fairness of the projects submitted with respect to the strategic objectives is confirmed for all ATS.

Finally, in analysing the outcome of the evaluation, Table 4.7 presents all the projects approved – projects which will therefore receive funding from the RL – compared to the total number of projects submitted. Overall, there are substantial differences between the various territories: 90% of projects submitted by the Local Area Plans within the ATS of Pavia were approved; between 50% and 70% of the projects submitted by Local Area Plans of the ATS of Brescia, Brianza, Milan and

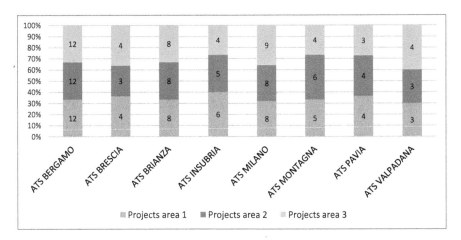

Fig. 4.5 Type of projects. Division according to ATS

Table 4.7 Final outcome of
the evaluation process

	Projects approved	Projects rejected
ATS BERGAMO	17	19
ATS BRESCIA	8	3
ATS BRIANZA	14	10
ATS INSUBRIA	7	8
ATS MILANO	18	7
ATS MONTAGNA	7	8
ATS PAVIA	10	1
ATS VALPADANA	7	3
	88	**59**

Valpadana were approved; while less than half of the projects submitted by the Local Area Plans of ATS Bergamo, Insubria and Montagna were approved.

What emerges from this analysis is a clear cut difference in design capacity in the various territories that could be determined by various factors: (a) difficulty on the part of the Local Area Plan administration in designing projects; (b) a lack of interest from the political/technical side in this second step of the DGR; (c) absence of support from the ATS; and, (d) general difficulties on the part of the Local Area Plan's administrative staff in putting together effective competitive calls for funding.

The reasons for not approving the projects mainly concern the failure to comply with the assessment requirements, the inadequacy of the project to comply with the general goals and finally, in some cases, the fact that the projects presented were already being co-financed by other actors (i.e. local or national foundations).

4.4.3   A Qualitative Point of View and Conclusions

If we look at the projects according to (broader) areas of action, we discover that the Local Area Plans have well defined priorities. The main sector is that dedicated to families and youth which accounts for 33% of the projects, followed by disability with 25%, services for elderly with 17%, action against social exclusions (fight against poverty and unemployment) with 16%, and finally housing that represents 9% of the total. Finally almost 40% of the projects present a multi-sectorial approach, with a main target individuated in one of the previously listed areas but one that is also closely interconnected to other policy sectors.

In Table 4.8 we have listed a series of projects (four for every area) that, in our opinion, are particularly interesting both in their general aims and the innovative aspects employed. The distribution according to policy area confirms the scattering calculated on the aggregated data, which places projects dedicated to family/minors and the disabled at the top of the Local Area Plans' concerns regarding strategic planning. As far as disability is concerned emphasis is placed on improving individual autonomy (where possible), educational skills and enforcing social ties so as to prevent or hamper the risk of social exclusion for people with disabilities. For this reason the disabled person is considered in connection with their own familiar and social context, so a multidimensional answer to his needs can be provided that includes planning interventions on a medium-long-term range (following a cultural path opened by the *Dopo di Noi* policy measure, which deals with the future of people with severe disabilities from a long term point of view, and plans measures and arrangements aimed at supporting the individual after the death of the relatives who take care of them). An interesting insight is represented by the presence of projects whose main aim is the definition of innovative policies able to give relief to the families of people with severe disabilities who act as care givers (i.e. Valle Brembana).

Foster care and child protection result among the most sensitive areas of action for the Local Area Plans, both in terms of the creation of common and standardised practices and in the definition of innovative courses of action for the protection of minors. This represents a huge topic for municipalities both because of the financial costs involved in placing minors in protected structures and because of the need to define practices better able to fit the multiple needs of minors who are victims of abuse, violence or difficult socioeconomic conditions. The number of minors in these situations is growing year after year (Autorità garante dell'infanzia 2015), and poses a structural question for municipalities, Local Area Plans and regions as to the kind of answer to give to such a multifaceted problem. Here the actions are considered innovative both for the changes introduced in well-established action models and for the structural involvement of societal actors (associations, the Third Sector, schools etc.).

The main element that connects almost all the 15 selected projects is the necessity to improve, enforce or even create a real homogeneity in the delivery of services within the Local Area Plan. This is quite interesting because only one of the Plans is new according to the criteria of the Decree No. 7631; this confirms a certain dif-

Table 4.8 Different examples of (approved) innovative projects (divided according to type of project and policy area)

Local Area Plan	Type of project	Project	Policy Area
Garbagnate	1	Homogeneous sharing for all Municipalities of the Local Area Plan, on an experimental basis, of the economic support to the assistance and care services guaranteed by "family carers" (*Assistenti familiari*) regularly employed by citizens in poor economic conditions.	Family and youth
Seregno	1	Definition of the requirements for access, participation in services and interventions in favour of minors and their families, protected meetings, regulation of relationships, foster care and insertion into communities that are uniform for all the municipalities of the Local Area Plan	Family and youth
Vimercate	2	Child protection (foster care). The project aims to identify common methods and tools in response to the procedural and instrumental dishomogeneity in the offer provided by the single municipalities of the Local Area Plan. The project will define the main operational procedures and instruments for identifying criteria of appropriateness and correct evaluation of the professional assistance intervention.	Family and youth
Lomellina	3	Provide a homogenous and common answer to: the need to protect minors in situations of prejudice, activation of training and comparison courses aimed at identifying and adequately addressing the problems involving minors with particular reference to the methods of reporting to the Judicial Authority also through the sharing of vademecum/best practices among the directly interested public-private actors (Municipal Social Services, Public and Private Schools, Third Sector, etc.).	Family and youth
Valle Brembana	3	Creation of psychoeducational support spaces for caring relatives of people with dementia (care giver). The project foresees the realisation of interventions to support the Care Giver, provide training and information interventions, and periodic home monitoring.	Family and youth
Valle Seriana/ Albino	1	Definition of a homogeneous regulation on acquired disability. The project aims to manage the responses to the educational-assistance needs of people with acquired disability and their families. Taking care of people with acquired disability, post hospital assistance, is a phase that weigh mainly on the resources of each family. These needs are only rarely addressed to the municipalities' Social Service, which usually provides fragmented responses through the adaptation of services aimed at the elderly or people with congenital disabilities.	Disability

(continued)

Table 4.8 (continued)

Local Area Plan	Type of project	Project	Policy Area
Cremona	2	Personal Autonomy Service: innovative tools for young disabled. All municipalities, third sector actors and schools are involved. Experimentation with new tools for detecting needs in order to orient the interventions provided for in the Support and Assistance Plan, experimenting with a path of taking charge and new ways of offering the service. Evaluation of individual outcomes on an electronic platform by the children's families.	Disability
Bassa Bresciana	2	Home care assistance. New quality criteria for the design and appropriateness of interventions: the welfare budget model.	Disability/ Family and youth
Desio	2	Reduction of complexity and fragmentation for the access to social assistance services for fragile subjects and their families. The goal will be reached through the integration of different policy areas, and the experimentation of new organisational models to respond with (in coordination with all the social offer units of the disability area).	Disability
Brescia Est	3	Interventions to promote autonomy for people with disabilities through new experimentations in the supply chain of services. Support to families with young disabled people in the transition from school to adult life.	Disability
Lodi	3	Learning difficulties of children in families with economic/social fragilities. An experimental intervention for the early identification of learning difficulties in the school context, through the training of teachers/educators and improving the filter for referral to social services.	Fight against social exclusion
Garbagnate	3	Development of a project (financed by a bank foundation), together with the third sector, aimed at bringing out informal groups of citizens of the area, who want to cooperate to build new forms of collective response to individual needs, oriented to the enforcement of individual economic condition (by the means of savings/reduction/ barterfeit), the contrast of the widespread condition of loneliness and isolation and the construction of bonds of solidarity and proximity, the redevelopment of places for collective use.	Fight against social exclusion

(continued)

Table 4.8 (continued)

Local Area Plan	Type of project	Project	Policy Area
Romano di Lombardia	2	Customer 2.0. Assessment of service quality, output, feedback and outcome The need is to strengthen the evaluation aspects of the services provided by the SAD (home care assistance). It includes the definition of a new governance model for the service with the definition of a unitary control room (Cabina di Regia); the analysis, in a logic of improvement, of the procedures and evaluation tools adopted by the managing bodies; the experimentation of new evaluation tools; the evaluation of the experimentation and the production of operational documentation; the evaluation of the general outcomes of the service.	Elderly
Rho	1	Homogenised regulations for access to residential services for the elderly. The involvement of all the municipalities in the area and stakeholders is foreseen. The project phases include the analysis of the standard costs of residential facilities for the elderly, the definition of the access criteria, the ISEE thresholds and the share of social-healthcare expenditure	Elderly
Menaggio	1	Implementation of a social housing service aimed at all evicted citizens or in housing emergency and to citizens affected by situations of poverty and fragility. To this end, a new framework regulation that includes requirements of homogeneous access for this service will be defined.	Housing/ Fight against social exclusion

ficulty, also in established Local Area Plans, in reducing the endemic fragmentation that characterises regional welfare. The reduction of fragmentation can be related both to the integration of different services (Desio) and to the redefinition of the flux/management of financial resources, which moves towards an integrated budget instead of confirming the persistent fragmentation of multiple intervention streams dedicated to a single user (Bassa Bresciana). From this point of view, the attempt made by single Local Area Plans (i.e. Valle Seriana) to improve the coordination within the healthcare dimension, one of the main problems affecting the RL system, is also significant. For this reason it is worth underlining just how important the effort is that emerges from all the selected projects to create/enforce a broad network better able to involve all the territorial actors (potentially) involved in the realisation/implementation of the policies (we can define it as structural data).

In conclusion, the majority of the Local Area Plans constituted by 31 December 2019 actively participated in the selection for the second award tranche; only a quarter of them did not submit projects, with significant differences found between the territories of the various ATS. The participating Local Area Plans usually submitted two or more projects that met the strategic objectives set out by the regional decree. This is confirmed by a comparison between the various ATS. On the whole, however, it emerges that 40% of the projects submitted, after careful analysis and requests for integrations, were not approved/financed because they did not meet the specific requirements set out by the Region. In this case too there is a significant difference from area to area. The regional government's new approach (monetary rewards and definition of policy targets) provides mixed evidence. While it has been ineffective in stimulating aggregation between a relevant number of Local Area Plans and a better rationalisation of a fragmented frame, it has proved to be an extremely useful tool for reflecting on the way in which Local Area Plans work. This has in fact contributed to bringing to light at least four orders of issues that raise questions about the functionality of the Local Area Plan:

(a) the interesting planning ability of a certain number of Local Area Plans that have worked on the response to new needs/social risks with innovative methods and/or with a multi sectorial approach, thus strengthening the effort to define new integrated policies;
(b) the difficulty of a large number of Local Area Plans (40%) in defining and planning structured projects;
(c) a certain territorial heterogeneity that coincides, roughly speaking, with the territorial area defined by the ATS boundaries;
(d) a certain delay in Local Area Plans that have been established for almost 20 years in reaching strategic and essential goals like the definition of homogenous criteria in all the involved municipalities for citizens' access to social services;
(e) the persistent need of Local Area Plans to reduce fragmentation along all the different lines which social policies involve (resources, actors, knowledge, data interoperability, policy actions), and,
(f) a certain difficulty in defining instruments useful for the evaluation of policy outcomes.

This analysis gives us a composite picture, which shows a large variance among Lombardy's territories that differ from making a great push towards innovation – both in governance and policy terms – to being substantially immobile and resistant to change. As stated before this immobilism can be connected to a series of variables like a persistent resistance to change from the public administration sector, difficulty in embracing innovative practices, structural limits in governance instruments dedicated to territorial coordination, stalemate among actors (joint decision trap) and a certain "parochial" approach in inter-municipal courses of action that consider routinized procedures as the best options from which it would be a mistake to move away (path dependence). Furthermore, we also have to stress the difficulties regional agencies have in boosting effective cooperation, especially as regards more incisive actions dedicated to the enforcement of integration, in particular among social and healthcare actions.

References

Agostini, C. (2008). Differenziazione e frammentazione territoriale delle politiche sociali. *Quaderni di Sociologia, 48*, 57–69. https://doi.org/10.4000/qds.833.
Aldag, A. M., & Warner, M. (2018). Cooperation, not cost savings: Explaining duration of shared service agreements. *Local Government Studies, 44*(3), 350–370. https://doi.org/10.1080/0300 3930.2017.1411810.

Autorità garante dell'infanzia. (2015). *La tutela dei minori in comunità.* https://www.garantein-fanzia.org/sites/default/files/la_tutela_dei_minorenni_in_comunita.pdf [first access 15 April 2020].

Barberis, E., Bergmark, A., & Minas, R. (2010). Rescaling processes in Europe: Convergence and divergence patterns towards multilevel governance? In Y. Kazepov (Ed.), *Rescaling social policies: Towards multilevel governance in Europe* (pp. 367–388). Ltd: Ashgate Publishing.

Battistella, A., De Ambrogio, U., & Ranci Ortigosa, E. U. D. (2004). *Il piano di zona: costruzione, gestione, valutazione.* Roma: Carocci Editore.

Bel, G., & Warner, M. E. (2016). Factors explaining inter-municipal cooperation in service delivery: A meta-regression analysis. *Journal of Economic Policy Reform, 19*(2), 91–115. https://doi.org/10.1080/17487870.2015.1100084.

Cajaiba-Santana, G. (2014). Social innovation: Moving the field forward. A conceptual framework. *Technological Forecasting and Social Change, 82*, 42–51. https://doi.org/10.1016/j.techfore.2013.05.008.

Champion, C., & Bonoli, G. (2011). Institutional fragmentation and coordination initiatives in western European welfare states. *Journal of European Social Policy, 21*(4), 323–334. https://doi.org/10.1177/0958928711412220.

Da Roit, B., & Sabatinelli, S. (2005). Il modello mediterraneo di welfare tra famiglia e mercato. *Stato e mercato, 25*(2), 267–290. https://doi.org/10.1425/20483.

Gori, C. (Ed.). (2018). *Il welfare delle riforme? Le politiche lombarde tra norme ed attuazione.* Rimini: Maggioli.

Gualini, E. (2006). The rescaling of governance in Europe: New spatial and institutional rationales. *European Planning Studies, 14*(7), 881–904. https://doi.org/10.1080/09654310500496255.

Kazepov, Y., & Barberis, E. (2013). *Il welfare frammentato. Le articolazioni regionali delle politiche sociali italiane.* Roma: Carocci.

Lumino, R., & Pirone, F. (2013). I sistemi regionali di assistenza sociale: governance, organizzazione dei servizi, strumenti e modalità operative. In Y. Kazepov & E. Barberis (Eds.), *Il welfare frammentato: Le articolazioni regionali delle politiche sociali italiane.* Roma: Carocci.

Madama, I. (2008). Regionalizzazione e politiche socio-assistenziali. *La rivista delle politiche sociali, 3*, 289–312.

Previtali, P., & Salvati, E. (2019). Social planning and local welfare. The experience of the Italian area social plan. *International Planning Studies, 24*(2), 180–194. https://doi.org/10.1080/13563475.2018.1528864.

Ranci, C., & Popolizio, M. (2013). L'impatto del federalismo fiscale sull'assetto del sistema integrato dei servizi sociali. In Y. Kazepov & E. Barberis (Eds.), *Il welfare frammentato: Le articolazioni regionali delle politiche sociali italiane.* Roma: Carocci.

Salvati, E. (2016). Governance e organizzazione dei nove Piani di Zona della provincia di Pavia. Un'analisi comparata. In P. in Previtali & P. Favini (Eds.), *L'organizzazione dei Piani di Zona in provincia di Pavia* (pp. 119–170). Pavia: Pavia University Press.

Salvati, E. (2020). Riorganizzare il welfare locale. Il modello del governance network e l'esperienza dei Piani di Zona lombardi. *Studi Organizzativi, 1*, 67–92. https://doi.org/10.3280/SO2020-001003.

Saruis, T., Colombo, F., Barberis, E., & Kazepov, Y. (2019). Istituzioni del welfare e innovazione sociale: un rapporto conflittuale? *Italian Journal of Social Policy, 1*, 23–38.

Silva, P., Teles, F., & Ferreira, J. (2018). Intermunicipal cooperation: The quest for governance capacity? *International Review of Administrative Sciences, 84*(4), 619–638. https://doi.org/10.1177/0020852317740411.

Chapter 5
The Difficult Path Towards Change

Abstract The Decree No. 7631/2017 does not represent an example of policy success because only a limited number of Local Area Plans have decided to take advantage of the opportunity of defining a new district area and move towards an aggregation. In light of the theoretical and analytical framework presented in the book, in this chapter we will try to assess and explain the conditions that have made some aggregations successful. The idea at the basis of this analysis is that there was a combination of pre-determined conditions that were fundamental to bringing about new forms of stricter and more institutionalised arrangements for inter-municipal cooperation. This empirical effort represents a useful contribution to the literature focused on the analysis of models of intermunicipal cooperation, reflecting on which are the (structural) favourable conditions that may lead towards governance changes in order to improve the degree of coordination and cooperation.

Keywords Intermunicipal cooperation · Local area plan · Organization · Social policies · Management · Reform · Local governance

5.1 Explaining the Cases of *Local Area Plan* Reorganisational Success

As outlined in the previous chapter, the application of Decree No. 7631/2017 has been far from being a success. Only a limited number of Local Area Plans have even considered the opportunity of defining a new district area and of this group only a small part has decided to move towards an aggregation. In light of the theoretical and analytical framework presented in the book – and keeping in mind the structural problems, shortcomings and the difficulties outlined in the previous chapter – we will now try to assess and explain the conditions that have made some aggregations successful. The idea at the basis of this analysis is that there was a combination of pre-determined conditions that were fundamental to bringing about new forms of stricter and even more institutionalised arrangements for inter-municipal cooperation (see Chap. 2). These new aggregations moved in the direction of enforcing the governance and institutional aspects concerning cooperation, and paved the way for

P. Previtali, E. Salvati, *Local Welfare and the Organization of Social Services*,
https://doi.org/10.1007/978-3-030-66128-1_5

91

defining new and more effective models of coordination and cooperation (which, as we now know, have a multidimensional implication due to the fact that they involve many different aspects like resources, knowledge, actors etc.). Such aggregations aim to enforce the institutionalisation of the governance environment in which numerous interactions among different and various local authorities and societal actors take place. These strengthened aggregations tend to favour the integration of different policies and the different policy networks that distinguish the policy production defined through networks (Fedele and Moini 2007).

Such favourable conditions have paved the way for the new aggregations but have obviously operated in different ways, due to territorial peculiarities and differences that – as we have seen in the previous chapters – are the endogenous elements that were affecting the development of the welfare state and social policies in Italy, and which led to its regional structural fragmentation (Agostini 2008; Ferrera 2008; Kazepov and Barberis 2013; Saruis et al. 2019).

This analysis is the result of the combination of different data sources. Five cases stood out as being particularly relevant to our research purposes (as exemplar cases) and were accessible to researchers, both in terms of interviews and direct participation in (some) preparatory and working meetings. The interview outcomes were triangulated, also taking into account other data sources: reports and official written documents, archival materials, reports, direct participation in workshops and organisational meetings, and field notes taken after formal and informal meetings. The interviews and the meeting participations were carried out between May 2018 and January 2020, and were analysed according to a chronological description for each single observed case study (Collier 2011). Semi-structured questions were used throughout the interviews, for a total number of 53 interviews. The interviewees were chosen because of their role in the policy process: the policy makers (officials of the RL), the territorial agencies who are in charge of supporting the policy implementation (Directors and officials of local health agencies), and the subjects that have to realise the reform (municipalities and *Local Area Plans*). All this different data enabled us to reconstruct the path of the reform and build a chronological analysis for every single case. Using process tracing in order to reveal and explain this path and its effectiveness, we focused on causal-process observations, and payed great attention to description as a key heuristic element useful for emphasising the causal sequence in which we are interested (Collier 2011; Beach and Pedersen 2019).

Unfortunately, it was not possible to examine and consider the new Local Area Plans of Oglio Po and Voghera due to the lack of available and comparable data.

5.2   Case Studies: The Troubled Application of the Decree No. 7631/2017

While in the previous chapter we focused on the motivations which can (partially) explain the resistance to change in the majority of Local Area Plans, in this chapter we would like to stress the elements that have led to positive organisational change in the governance arrangements of some *areas*. First, there are some questions which should be answered: what has influenced the effectiveness of Decree No. 7631/2017? Under which territorial conditions have the law provisions led to success or to failure? Is it possible to "learn" both from the causes of failure and of success, and so provide useful insights for academics and practitioners?

As previously explained, aware of the territorial diversifications in the social sector and a general difficulty, as revealed over the years, in recomposing this governance differentiation, the regional government gave the Local Area Plans different time frames in which to define the new *district*.

In the first time frame provided by the regional government we found only three aggregations among Local Area Plans while all the remaining 45 Local Area Plans supported by municipalities were already existing inter-municipal agreements which fulfilled the defined inhabitants' threshold.

These limited numbers and such marginal outcomes, despite the monetary incentive, demonstrate to what extent the voluntary aggregation has been a substantial failure. The opportunity of directly overseeing some of these aggregation processes, gave us the chance to analyse the factors that have stimulated or limited cooperation. This provided us with a unique point of view of the aggregation process, both as concerns the decisions made by the actors involved and as concerns the organisational models applied to overcome potential and actual obstacles to integration.

To empirically examine the conditions that have prompted this output, we will use the dimensions introduced through our theoretical framework. In this chapter we will present the five case studies investigated (Fig. 5.1): for all the cases we will analyse the defined indicators in order to understand which conditions can influence a policy reform in the field. Table 5.1 presents the indicators used in the theoretical framework which were chosen for their usefulness in clearly reconstructing the entire process which led to the new aggregations.

For each case study, the conditions preliminary to the aggregation process will be presented, employing a process tracing approach, so as to draw a precise picture of the context. With reference to the aforementioned indicators, the various sections that follow will reconstruct the aggregation process, with an emphasis on the enabling conditions and on the hurdles. In the end some concluding comparative remarks will be presented, in order to highlight the regularities that may have acted as a fly-wheel for success.

5.2.1   Local Area Plans of the Lomellina: Vigevano-Garlasco-Mortara

The three Local Area Plans of Garlasco, Mortara and Vigevano agreed in June 2018 to dissolve their own previous inter-municipal agreements in order to create a unique Local Area Plan called *Ambito della Lomellina* (from the name of the geographical area to which all the municipalities belong to) (Table 5.2). The process

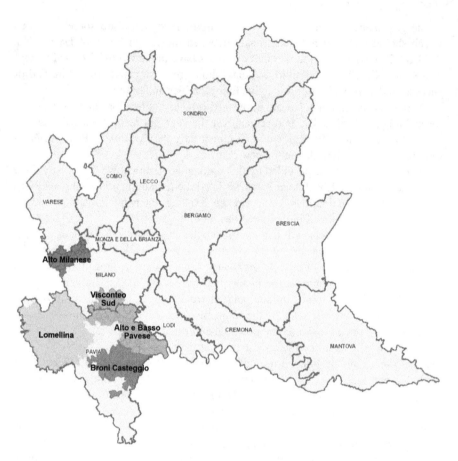

Fig. 5.1 New Area Local Plans in Lombardy

started in February 2018 on the initiative of the Presidents of the Mayor Assemblies of Garlasco and Vigevano who decided to take advantage of the opportunity offered by the regional government. After an initial period of uncertainty and a couple of joint meetings led by the ATS Pavia with the support of the University, the Local Area Plan of Mortara also agreed to join the new network.

The political homophily of the three leading mayors played a clear role in overcoming some initial doubts and enabling a broad and shared agreement to be reached. The mayor of Vigevano (the largest city of the area) in particular played an important role in convincing the mayor of Mortara of the feasibility of the project. The mayor of Mortara was the most sceptical about the operability of a future Local Area Plan of such huge dimensions, in particular as regards the coordination of many municipalities (the great part of which is of small dimension). The main driver that stimulated the three political leaderships of the previous Local Area Plans was the opportunity of creating a homogeneous integrated territory from what were extremely fragmented territories, with the ambition of providing a new organisa-

Table 5.1   The path towards aggregation

	Lomellina	Visconteo Sud	Broni-Casteggio	Alto Milanese	Alto e Basso Pavese
Structure Size and number of municipalities Strong vs weak ties Level of trust Political Homophily	Many municipalities (50) from three previous pds. Majority are small municipalities except for one big city Strong ties, many previous working and planning relationships, with a shared geographical and cultural identity (Lomellina) High level of trust among municipalities, politicians and administrative officers Strong political homophily between mayors	Few municipalities, only one large (Rozzano) the majority are of medium dimensions (between 5.001–15.000 inhabitants) with a relevant degree of homogeneity Strong ties, many pre-existing relationships on projects and services Extremely high level of trust among bureaucrats No political homophily	High number of municipalities of small dimensions Strong ties created by years of formal and informal cooperation, with some pre-existing relationships, Good level of trust (high between administrative officials, medium among politicians) No political Homophily	Limited number of municipalities, quite similar for number of inhabitants, with only one big city. Complexity augmented by the presence of two Azienda *Speciale* which are public companies that produce and supply social services, Weak ties, some pre-existing relationships concerning projects Medium level of trust No political homophily	High number of municipalities of small dimensions Weak ties, No pre-existing relationships Scarce level of trust No political Homophily

(continued)

Table 5.1 (continued)

	Lomellina	Visconteo Sud	Broni-Casteggio	Alto Milanese	Alto e Basso Pavese
Process (workshop, Plans, committees, meetings, etc.)	The role of Vigevano – the biggest city – as driver for the aggregation Few organisational meetings, many formal and informal relationships, support from University as network orchestrator (in a second phase)	Plans, meetings, working groups, joint committee	Many political and technical meetings. No public meetings and just one meeting with the Third Sector (at the end of the process). Working groups and support from the University of Pavia as network orchestrator (in a second phase)	At the beginning Legnano seemed not to be interested (the big city which refused the aggregation with smaller towns) Few meetings, limited coordination processes	No structured meetings and working groups, except for a couple of meetings involving both politicians and bureaucrats Strategy and structure (request to the University of Pavia for a cost-benefit analysis) Disruptive Power of decision
Actors	Strong political leadership exerted by mayors as "sponsor". Administrative officers with a positive role. Support from non-profit organisations which act as "catalyst". Support from the University of Pavia as network orchestrator and "champion"	Administrative officers as" implementers" and sponsor of the aggregation.	Presence of a doubtful political leadership. Administrative officers with a positive role	University of Pavia as "orchestrator" and" champion". Presence of the political leadership	In a first phase, political leadership and administrative officers, with a negative role. In a second phase direct presence of the political leadership. Support from the University of Pavia as network orchestrator and "champion"

(continued)

Table 5.1 (continued)

	Lomellina	Visconteo Sud	Broni-Casteggio	Alto Milanese	Alto e Basso Pavese
Barriers	None. Good level of propensity towards change from the administrative sector.	None High level of propensity towards change from the administrative sector	Some initial doubts from the political actors. Good level of propensity towards change from the administrative sector	Barriers are constructed within the governmental organisation itself. Good level of propensity towards change from the administrative sector	Barriers are constructed within the governmental organisation itself. Stop to innovation due to the embedded discourses about governance (role of path dependence and defence of the status quo) Framing of a situation as a race to reach a deadline Cover-up strategies
Performance	Excellent: perfect timing and an agreement easily reached by mayors	Excellent: central role played by the administrative side	Initial stand by period, in a second phase a fresh start and a very good output	Initial stand by period, in a second phase a fresh start. Complicated output	Failure in a first phase, followed by a long stand by period. Rapid restart in the last weeks of 2019 and a complicated output. Consistent risks of disintegration and/or inefficiency in the future

tional model capable of providing new services and gaining external resources. As stated by Vigevano's mayor "*a new territorial integration and a scale which enables the planning and supply capacity of the 50 municipalities involved in the project to be improved*". It is interesting to underline that the political leadership of Vigevano's Local Area Plan, despite the fact that they already fulfilled the population target

Table 5.2 Local Area Plans Lomellina (before and after)

Local Area Plans	No. of municipalities	Tot. Inhabitants	New Local Area Plans	No. of municipalities	Tot. Inhabitants
Garlasco	27	55.100	Ambito della Lomellina	51	180.358
Mortara	20	42.108			
Vigevano	4	83.150			

required by the decree and so did not need to pursue a new agreement, have led the path towards integration from the beginning.

Agreement among the political parts was quite straightforward from the beginning of the process, thanks to the desire of all the actors to conclude the new inter-municipal agreement before the end of June, in time for the first window of opportunity. The three administrative sectors started work immediately on the new organisational arrangement with a high level of effectiveness that was the result of a long tradition of working cooperation between the three previous Local Area Plans: a cooperation that started at the beginning of 2000, and that led to the definition of common projects in social services production (formal cooperation) and established a consolidated experience of exchange (informal cooperation). Despite a situation characterised by an extremely high level of administrative fragmentation with 50 municipalities in the new network, of which 41 very small with less than 5000 inhabitants, the path toward a successful application of the decree, has been possible due to the coordination efforts of the political leaderships who have worked to boost mutual trust and reduce uncertainty among the participants and tried to create as clear a framework as possible for cooperation. From an organisational point of view, the new *area* decided to opt for the classical UdP arrangement, with a fairly centralised structure from which to immediately start a homogenisation process with regards to practice, funds management, services supply, human resource allocation etc. In order to reduce the inefficiency and ineffectiveness risks produced by the presence of 50 members, the new Local Area Plan decided to create an intermediate arena (the *tavolo tecnico-politico*) composed of a pool of representatives of the mayors supported by the administrative sector, whose job was to provide preliminary reflections on the dossiers, define the agenda setting and formalise proposals for the assembly. In the first months this governance instrument proved to be quite efficient in speeding up the decisional process and avoiding the risks of the so-called joint decision trap (Scharpf 1988), by providing a useful arena for informal agreements. This action was made possible by the longstanding collaboration between the administrative and political sectors of the Local Area Plans. Furthermore, this consolidated cooperation proved to be useful in easily overcoming some aspects of resistance to change both in the administrative and political sectors (especially in the former Local Area Plans of Mortara), and in assuring the new network some routinized models of cooperation able to limit the risks of agency loss and uncertainty.

The creation of the new inter-municipal governance model was also supported by the external aid of the University researchers who cooperated directly with the administrative officers to provide a detailed action plan. In this scenario the high level of trust, the strong pre-existing relationships, the leadership role exerted by politicians and the role of University as an external consultant have all played a decisive role in the successful fulfilment of the task.

5.2.2   Local Area Plans Visconteo Sud

The two Local Area Plans of Rozzano and Pieve Emanuele were extremely different both in terms of size and complexity. Rozzano's Local Area Plan was composed of 4 municipalities of which one was extremely large (more than 40.000 inhabitants) and three were of a medium dimension (between 5.001 and 15.000 inhabitants). Instead Pieve Emanuele's Local Area Plan was composed of 7 municipalities of which 4 were of a medium dimension (between 5.001–15.000 inhabitants) and three extremely small (less than 5.000 inhabitants) (Table 5.3). This state of affairs has unavoidably led over time to the definition of two different models of governance, budgetary arrangements and service production/supply, in order to cope with the different needs expressed by the two networks. Despite these structural differences the two Local Area Plans were able, in the past, to establish a strong and routinised cooperation – facilitated by a similar population structure, with comparable social risks and needs – which had led to a joint working model between the two administrative offices. The discussion about the feasibility of a new and broader inter-municipal agreement has involved both the political and the administrative sides through single and joint meetings. Our interviews reveal that the result has been the firm belief that *"the aggregation process and the creation of a new network could represent a useful opportunity to developing the social services supply in the territory. This opportunity will only work if the definition of the new governance system respects some gradualist criteria and preserves the good aspects of the previous experiences"*. The two political leaderships were characterised by homophily, an element which definitely helped in the initial stages of considering the project's feasibility. Furthermore from our interviews the idea emerged that this choice was not taken simply as compliance to a law, but *"as a way to coordinate and share positive and valuable administrative experiences, organisational models and services which then become a common asset for the new network, giving citizens the opportunity to choose among different and effective services, and in so doing create an added value compared to the simple sum of the two previous inter-municipal agreements"*.

Table 5.3   Local Area Plans Ambito Visconteo Sud Milano (before and after)

Local Area Plans	No. of municipalities	Tot. Inhabitants	New Local Area Plans	No. of municipalities	Tot. Inhabitants
Rozzano	4	74.447	Ambito Visconteo Sud Milano	11	125.699
Pieve Emanuele	7	51.252			

Even before the approbation of the decree the two Assemblies of Mayors started a path of cooperation which resulted in a series of joint meetings between the two, in order to share reflections on the common needs, problems and opportunities for cooperation. For this reason the two Assemblies in March 2018, asked their administrative offices to prepare a study of the pros and cons of a merger between the two Local Area Plans, and to formulate a plan for a new governance arrangement. This assignment started a phase of study in which all the aspects concerning the function of the two Local Area Plans were analysed: this phase ended with the drafting of a document, produced by a joint committee, which concluded that the creation of a new inter-municipal agreement could be accepted due to the great commonality in the actions and organisational models of the two Local Area Plans. Furthermore, the committee also demonstrated the potential benefits this merger would produce, including how by applying additional effort in some strategic areas like more effective specialised services, and the empowerment of specific social policy, it would be possible to gain more power and strength when confronting other institutional actors. The final output – the creation of a new inter-municipal network – was reached thanks to the presence of well-defined elements similar to those that led to Lomellina's success: a well-informed political leadership that pushed for the result and operated to reduce uncertainty, and good previous inter-organisational collaboration associated with a very low degree of resistance to change from the administrative offices. The presence of an external network orchestrator was less relevant than in the Lomellina case, because the support was concentrated in the final part of the process, i.e. the redaction of the agreement.

Finally, like in the Lomellina case, the decision was made to move towards a substantial and quick homogenisation of the two former Local Area Plans, without an intermediate period of separate management of funds and services. In order to speed up the new organisation, the two administrative sectors prepared a timetable concerning the steps needed to move forward to the new Local Area Plan, indicating – for example – the date of conclusion of the outstanding contracts for externalised services, and the definition of a single agreement with the Third Sector in order to prepare the new unified organisation. The Visconteo Sud experience is paradigmatic of the central role that trust and strong pre-existing cooperation relationships play in creating a favourable environment for the reform's success.

5.2.3   Local Area Plans Broni-Casteggio

The *Ambito* of Broni-Casteggio was one of the last to be formed. This is quite interesting because the two previous Local Area Plans of Broni and Casteggio were extremely similar in their features and organisational arrangements. Both of them had a high level of municipal fragmentation with many (extremely) small municipalities and two larger cites that exerted leadership over the Local Area Plans (the cities of Broni and Casteggio) (Table 5.4). Both have a peculiar geography consisting of both flat and hilly areas (where the majority of the small municipalities are

Table 5.4 Local Area Plans Broni- Casteggio (before and after)

Local Area Plans	No. of municipalities	Tot. Inhabitants	New Local Area Plans	No. of municipalities	Tot. Inhabitants
Broni	25	39.585	Ambito Broni-Casteggio	50	71.483
Casteggio	25	31.898			

located). The population of both Local Area Plans was quite elderly on average and so the main target of social services was substantially similar; the provision of home care services for old people. Moreover, the two administrative sectors share a long experience of collaboration and cooperation, supported by exchanges between the administrative personnel and officials and by the similarity of the two *areas* (which are also geographic neighbours).

Given this state of affairs, it would be natural to think that the aggregation process would be quick and easy. Instead the path has been characterised by numerous stops and starts, in which the hesitation and the doubts of the political parties have played a decisive role. This hesitation was not only the product of a political difference between the mayors of the largest municipalities, but also the result of limited trust between many of the involved mayors and the fear of losing not only "independence" but everything that had been created – and was considered efficient – in the two Local Area Plans. It took a long time and many political and administrative meetings, as well as working sessions with the ATS and the University of Pavia to convince all the reluctant political actors. Furthermore, in order to improve mutual trust, it was necessary to create governance mechanisms able to offer political guarantees to all the parties involved (an equal distribution of top leadership positions within the new Local Area Plans, the safeguard of the role of the two administrative sectors, a governance system able to preserve the peculiarities of the two previous Local Area Plans etc.). The "second half" of the reform process which passed the assurance regarding the new governance assets, helped the mayors of the two largest cities convince the reluctant actors to establish the new Local Area Plan. For the governance arrangements, differently from the Lomellina and Visconteo Sud experiences, the new *area* of Broni-Casteggio decided to define a less centralised organisational model. The governance is based on the UdP but the two territorial areas of the two Local Area Plans' funding have substantial autonomy in the definition of some specific services and in the management of part of the resources, and two autonomous territorial offices located in the headquarters of the two former Local Area Plans have been established. Broni and Casteggio also decided to create an intermediate body composed of representatives of the mayors' assembly but, differently from Lomellina, this body has larger amounts of power, resources and competences, and defines itself as a sort of "small mayors' assembly".

It is in this arena that the open and informal processes of conflict, bargaining and agreement among the mayors takes place who, substantially, continue to represent the two previously existing areas of Broni and Casteggio. Furthermore, all the top positions of the Local Area Plan's governance are filled by members selected to represent the two former areas of Broni and Casteggio. All these organisational and governance provisions are meant to guarantee cooperation, improve trust through the use of safeguarding tools and reduce the risk of agency loss and free riding, with the final aim of ensuring that neither of the two former Local Area Plans could prevail over the other. Only time will tell how effective this decision is, but the risk is that it could be subject to several problems in terms of effectiveness, the quality of policy making decisions, and the probability of falling into joint decision traps produced by multiple veto. The Broni-Casteggio case tells us something extremely interesting. It confirms the importance and centrality of the role exerted by the presence of mutual trust and by a positive attitude from the administrative officials. Moreover, it sheds light on the role of the "network orchestrator" played by other actors (University, ATS, etc.) which help to remove obstacles and create favourable conditions for an agreement. In this case, as explained by our theoretical framework on the role of networks, the decisive action was the definition of organisational/ governance arrangements able to safeguard all the actors' interests and roles by creating an environment which guaranteed institutionalised instruments of mutual assurance (and hopefully, tools able to increase the level of mutual trust).

5.2.4   Local Area Plan Alto Milanese

As far as the Castano and Legnano experiences are concerned, the main point of interest and of complication is the peculiarity of the organisational model applied by both the Local Area Plans for the supply of social services. The complexity in this case is not related to the issue of administrative and social fragmentation (because these territories are characterised by a medium level of fragmentation but a high level of heterogeneity among municipalities with large cities, medium sized towns and small villages) (Table 5.5) but is the by-product of the presence of two different *Aziende Speciali* operating in the two territories. The *Azienda Speciale* is a company thanks to which the municipalities externalise the production and supply of social services; they are 'independent' and complex organisations. In this case, as explicitly stated by the political leadership of the two Local Area Plans, neither of them was willing to give up its *Azienda Speciale*.

To overcome this issue, the political and administrative parts instituted a series of joint meetings with the aim of defining a solution based on dividing the tasks

Table 5.5 Local Area Plans Alto Milanese (before and after)

Local Area Plans	No. of municipalities	Tot. Inhabitants	New Local Area Plans	No. of municipalities	Tot. Inhabitants
Castano Primo	11	70.239	Ambito Alto Milanese	22	259.076
Legnano	11	188.837			

between the two *Aziende*, both of which will continue to provide services to their respective territories but which will be coordinated by a joint commission led by the political leadership. Despite the absence of previous inter-organisational collaborations between the two networks, the meetings produced a draft project for the reorganisation of the social services governance in the new network, which was able to disrupt a well rooted path dependence in the organisational arrangements and showed a significant degree of willingness to change. In this case, the actions of the ATS and the University of Pavia resulted extremely useful in removing some hurdles (mainly as regards the services management model rather than the planning phase or the governance instruments). The definition of a series of regular meetings – the *tavolo di programmazione zonale* – to overcome the shortcomings of such a complex fusion, define the organisational features of the new Local Area Plans and create the conditions for a "semi-permanent" brainstorming on the definition of policy priorities, has helped substantially to avoid deadlocks and reduce the risks connected to the absence of strong previous ties and mutual trust.

Despite the fact that the process has been slowed down by some stops and starts, the two Local Area Plans finally reached an agreement based on a governance model in which a high level of decision sharing among the actors is guaranteed and the roles of the two *Aziende* Speciali safeguarded, but at the same time there is an appreciable centralisation of the planning phase. Partially similar to the Broni-Casteggio case, Alto Milanese also decided to have a more decentralised arrangement of the Local Area Plans, although without the large margin defined by Broni. While the autonomy of the two *Aziende* was ensured and they can continue operating in accordance with the previous territorial sectors of competences, the UdP acts to coordinate their operations. So the UdP, in this new context, takes on an even greater role because it is effectively placed at the centre of the governance network and has the task of coordinating the various territorial and organisational experiences. In order to improve and enforce the degree of coordination and sharing, the positive experience of the *tavolo di programmazione zonale* led it to be upgraded to *tavolo di programmazione zonale e progettazione zonale*; the aim was to gather together all the actors of the net, and to encourage the direct participation of these actors in all the working phases of the Local Area Plan (analysis, planning, implementation, evaluation of the services). Like all the other areas, the functions of political input and control are in the hands of the *Assemblea dei Sindaci* which is supported by a narrower arena (like in Lomellina and Broni-Casteggio) called the *tavolo politico* composed of a pool of mayors who represent the two former Local Area Plans of Castano and Legnano, and the administrative sector. Like in the Broni-Casteggio experience and differently from Lomellina, this arena has a significant amount of direction and executive powers/competences: the coordination of the planning and management of the interventions to be implemented through the respective companies; ensuring links with other sectoral policies (work, school, home, etc.); strengthening relationships with Third Sector actors and social partners; and, safeguarding the functioning of the territorial governance system, the connection between the Local Area Plans' level and the individual Municipalities (and other forms of associated management which exist in the territory).

All these functions define the picture of a new Local Area Plan that, due to the complexity of the two founding actors, needed the definition of an arena dedicated to: (a) the safeguarding of some peculiarities of the two territories, (b) the improvement of effective network coordination (Salvati 2020), (c) the empowerment of mutual trust, (d) the definition of some sort of cooperation between multilevel actors/competencies (Kazepov 2010), and, (e) the resolution of governance dilemmas (Previtali and Salvati 2019). In this case the degree of uncertainty was not connected to administrative fragmentation or to the fear of destroying a well routinized working model, but instead was related to the decision to preserve the role of the two *Aziende Speciali*. The positive attitude of the administrative officers (both from municipalities and *Aziende Speciali*) and the role of the external network orchestrators, resulted decisive in removing the obstacles and creating a positive framework for cooperation and coordination able to guarantee the interests of the different actors involved. Of final note is the low number of barriers to the destruction of the previous administrative routine and a weak path dependency in bureaucratic courses of action thanks to a good propensity towards change.

5.2.5 Local Area Plans Alto e Basso Pavese

The case of *Certosa-Corteolona* is quite interesting because while the indicators pointed in different directions, the final output proved positive and resulted in the creation of a new Local Area Plan. The attempt made by the Local Area Plans of *Certosa* and *Cortelona* to define a common inter-municipal agreement is a paradigmatic example of a sum of hurdles and oppositions, a sort of 'benchmark' useful for understanding what the main conditions that could lead to failure are even when there is a kind of legal bond. Despite the fact that the two Local Area Plans have an extremely different total population size, they share a high level of fragmentation both in terms of the number and size of the involved municipalities (Table 5.6). In the Corteolona Local Area Plan only one municipality is over the 5.000 inhabitants while in Certosa there are six (here the 'largest town' has 8.500 inhabitants). In Corteolona the population was spread among small towns, and suffered problems of coordination and service delivery, while in Certosa the Local Area Plan's administrative office had a strong grasp on the services, with a supply model organised around a division of the territory into three/four areas of action (according to the type of service delivered) with a service coordinator in charge of supply.

Table 5.6 Local Area Plans Ambito Alto e Basso Pavese (before and after)

Local Area Plans	No. of municipalities	Tot. Inhabitants	New Local Area Plan	No. of municipalities	Tot. Inhabitants
Certosa	24	75.806	Alto e Basso Pavese	49	121.194
Cortelona	25	45.388			

Due to the different structure of the population, the two Local Area Plans had defined different core areas of action. Corteolona, with an elderly population, focused its efforts on services dedicated to the aged, while Certosa with a younger population – due also to the movement of families from the metropolitan area of Milan –dedicated more attention to the services for childhood and youth both in terms of prevention, and the care and fight against social exclusion (services like childhood care, fight against drugs/alcohol addiction, social inclusion, education, support for young unemployed etc.). Summing up, it is easy to see how different the two Local Area Plans were not only in organisational terms, but also in terms of their targets for the supply of social services. The political and bureaucratic parts of both the Local Area Plans were extremely sceptical about the feasibility of a common inter-municipal agreement and there was a relatively low level of mutual trust. The various formal and informal talks that took place – approximately – from summer 2018 to summer 2019, underlined the differences between the two Local Area Plans both in organisational and budgetary terms; the two administrative structures did not have any experience of relevant previous inter-organisational collaboration (either formal or informal). In the first round of talks both political leaderships demonstrated a lack of trust in their interlocutor, and had great difficulties determining which conditions would be valuable for reducing the uncertainty of the process. Many problems were found in terms of budget allocation and in the definition of new governance instruments, along with the fear of the smaller Local Area Plan (Corteolona) of being "absorbed" by Certosa instead of being an equal partner in the new agreement. Moreover, of note, was each Local Area Plan's fear of losing their respective established organisational models for the management of social interventions and routinised services, and their many doubts about the possibility of creating valuable instruments to reduce uncertainty. Differently from the political parties, the two administrative sectors proved to be more positive about defining a possible agreement, but effectively the acceptance of a reform delivered by a public policy at the level of an individual member in an organisation, proved to be insufficient for its successful implementation at the organisational level (Kumar et al. 2007). Furthermore, the direct presence on the 'field' of the University counsellors – in the first step – did not produce any concrete results, and they failed in their facilitation of the preliminary conditions for an agreement. From the beginning, resistance was quite striking and visible: with the willingness to change and modify rooted administrative and planning practices being almost absent.

Quite surprisingly a second round of talks led by the ATS with the support of the University, produced a shift in the previous positions. The two administrative sectors even showed an increased predisposition towards the feasibility of a new *Ambito* – which stemmed from the idea that in the near future the regional government could be prone to provide more support to the new *Ambiti* that resulted from an aggregation – and one of the two political sides decided to take a strong leadership role and become the driver of the process towards the final goal. In order to soften the different resistances, a plan concerning the governance of the new Local Area Plan was presented. In this report, the two former Local Area Plans were guaranteed a significant degree of autonomy, their different policy priorities were safeguarded and the identification of the first year of life of the new plan was proposed as a sort of "bridge period" in which the two parts could define the instruments and the organisational tools needed to boost coordination.

This model proposed a sort of "federative Local Area Plan", coordinated by the UdP which would oversee the administrative compliance and supply/production of social services, but with the two territories of Certosa and Corteolona preserving a certain degree of autonomy (they are officially recognised as territorial operative offices) in the definition of issue priorities and a subdivision of the resources based on the historical expenditure of the two former Local Area Plans and not on the services provided. Also in this case the creation of an intermediate structure, composed of 12 representatives of the two Local Area Plans (6 + 6), that fulfils the task of agenda setter for the Mayors Assembly and that promotes political bargaining and coordination between the two territories was approved. The key to the success of this complex experience can be traced back to the presence of three different elements: (a) a (new) stronger role exercised by external actors such as the network orchestrator, (b) the new centrality of one of the political actors that took on the leadership role and a more cooperative inclination towards the other part compared to the strong assertiveness of the past (an inclination that fed the fear of annexation instead of cooperation) and, (c) the definition of governance arrangements that ensured a relevant degree of autonomy to both parts. According to the organisational literature a positive effect towards change can be exerted by a successful experience of change and reform, which in turn can result in the diffusion of new practices (innovations) at both the individual and organisational levels (Conell and Cohn 1995). In this case the successful experience of other Local Area Plans in the same district (Lomellina and Broni-Casteggio) provided the evidence that a new and larger inter-municipal agreement could be reached and be effective, this acted as a boost to push the agreement in a positive direction.

The path of this new *Area* will probably be more complicated compared to the others. It will be particularly interesting to see if this partially centralised governance model can ensure an effective and efficient management of the Local Area Plan. Furthermore, it will be of paramount importance to understand if this cooperation can reinforce the actors' mutual trust, which at the moment seems to be less solid than in the other observed experiences. Probably all these issues will be influenced – positively or negatively – by the Local Area Plan's performances and by its capacity to satisfy the different needs and interests of the actors involved.

5.3   Insights Regarding the Process of Local Governance Reorganisation. What Have We Learnt About the Realisation of a Successful Path?

In order to individuate the conditions that have a positive effect on the successful realisation of a reform concerning the governance and the organisational aspects of inter-municipal cooperation in the field of social assistance, we carried out a qualitative study on the few Local Area Plans that have complied with the legislative indications. We have seen how complicated it can be to establish a new model of cooperation if some variables are missing or are rather weak. Among the various variables examined, we can underline in particular the role of:

- mutual trust;
- political will;
- ties and previous experience of cooperation;
- the role of a third party acting as network orchestrator.

In all the analysed experiences distinguished by rapid agreement and a low level of conflict, we can find the contextual presence of these three elements. The two most "complicated" processes of aggregation – Alto e Basso Pavese and Alto Milanese – were those processes in which mutual trust and/or previous experience were missing. Other variables like the size and number of municipalities and the mayors' political homophily proved to be of minor importance. The presence of a political leadership directly involved in the process, whose aim and effective will is to create the conditions necessary to reaching an agreement is a positive activator. This confirm some evidence produced by literature concerning intermunicipal cooperation in Italy that is that focused on how important is the presence of strong political will rather than, for example, the chance to take advantage of regional and state aid in making these types of cooperation effective (Fedele and Moini 2007).

Extremely interesting, independently from the positive output, are the results that emerge from the analyses of the paths towards the aggregation and the organisational/governance instruments set up for the aggregation. The cases which had a quicker and less tumultuous process – Lomellina and Visconteo Sud – are the ones in which the actors didn't need to provide specifically arranged arenas for bargaining and compensation and, furthermore, decided to move quickly forward towards an immediate (and as far as possible) homogenous governance arrangement for the new Local Area Plan. On the other hand, the cases characterised by difficulties, stops and starts, conflicts or low levels of trust among partners had to define governance instruments useful for limiting potential conflicts (Cristofoli et al. 2017), an arena of governance dedicated to direct bargaining between the territories (Salvati 2020) and to adopt a more decentralised organisational structure. This choice can be interpreted as a way of containing the governance of governance dilemma (Kazepov and Barberis 2013; Previtali and Salvati 2019), in order to insure against the possible defections and power asymmetries that feed conflicts.

The issue at stake is to understand if these governance provisions prove useful in avoiding disruptive conflicts and, moreover, whether or not they will lead to suboptimal outputs biased by joint decision traps and multiple veto players. These cases represent a sort of partial resistance to change, in which actors recognise the importance/utility/obligation of change but propose solutions that can limit, depending on their point of view and inclinations, the impact of this change on their organisational routine and the (perceived) negative influence on the management of their interests. The theory of the organisational fields dedicated to the process of restructuring, explains how, in the presence of change, pressures and external shocks, processes of re-composition and revision of interests, power structures and the definition of new cooperative relationships can lead to conflicts in an attempt to maintain the status quo, limit the impact of change and not lose power (Powell 1991). Our theoretical framework shows that the successful management of these conflicts depends heavily on the type of organisational arrangements that the actors/network institutionalised in order to pursue cooperation and coordination, and reduce defections, agency loss and ineffective systems. The main hurdles to remove have proved to be the resistance towards change in public administration, the political side's fear of losing control over part of their policy competences and the uncertainty about the possibility of creating a new organisational model able to work for an augmented number of partners.

We have seen that the presence of a third actor such as the network orchestrator can create the right conditions to overcome organisational problems, fine tune the activity of different actors and, furthermore, contribute to improving mutual trust among the actors (Kumar et al. 2007). As stated by Bartelings et al. (2017, p.357) "with the purpose of improving innovation and future value creation, such orchestrators are the liaising nerve centres of the network to bridge gaps between network partners". The shortcomings produced by a certain resistance to change can be overcome by the effective action of a political leadership that acts as a driver for change and by an external support able to (partially) curb a path dependence routine. The combined effects of these two actions are able to (at least partially) overcome part of the bureaucratical resistance to change. Another important leverage to removing obstacles produced by the administrative sector, is the assurance that their individual and institutional roles will not be hurt by an aggregative/change path.

It is in this way that successful innovation in inter-municipal cooperation is affected by the interaction of these different elements. If in broad terms the regional reforms proved to be ineffective due to the scarce number of Local Area Plans that decided to move towards change, it is important to point out that the actors that did decide to follow the path of aggregation have produced important insights into understanding how to improve inter-municipal coordination in a delicate sector like that of social policies. A sector that is multidimensional in the implication of the defined policies and that is multilevel and plural with regards to the actors, powers and competencies involved.

References

Agostini, C. (2008). Differenziazione e frammentazione territoriale delle politiche sociali. *Quaderni di Sociologia, 48*, 57–69. https://doi.org/10.4000/qds.833.

Bartelings, J., Goedee, J., Raab, J., & Bijl, R. (2017). The nature of orchestrational work. *Public Management Review, 19*(3), 342–360. https://doi.org/10.1080/14719037.2016.1209233.

Beach, D., & Pedersen, R. B. (2019). *Process-tracing methods: Foundations and guidelines.* University of Michigan Press.

Collier, D. (2011). Understanding process tracing. *PS: Political Science & Politics, 44*(4), 823–830. https://doi.org/10.1017/S1049096511001429.

Conell, C., & Cohn, S. (1995). Learning from other people's actions: Environmental variation and diffusion in French coal mining strikes, 1890-1935. *American Journal of Sociology, 101*(2), 366–403. https://doi.org/10.1086/230728.

Cristofoli, D., Meneguzzo, M., & Riccucci, N. (2017). Collaborative administration: The management of successful networks. *Public Management Review, 19*(3), 275–283. https://doi.org/10.1080/14719037.2016.1209236.

Fedele, M., & Moini, G. (2007). Italy: The changing boundaries of inter-municipal cooperation. In Hulst, R., & Van Montfort, A. (Eds.). *Inter-municipal cooperation in Europe ()*. Springer, Dordrecht, pp. 117–138.

Ferrera, M. (2008). Dal welfare state alle welfare regions: la riconfigurazione spaziale della protezione sociale in Europa. *La rivista delle politiche sociali, 3*(2008), 17–49.

Kazepov, Y. (Ed.). (2010). *Rescaling social policies: Towards multilevel governance in Europe.* Ashgate Publishing, Ltd.

Kazepov, Y., & Barberis, E. (2013). *Il welfare frammentato. Le articolazioni regionali delle politiche sociali italiane.* Roma: Carocci.

Kumar, S., Kant, S., & Amburgey, T. L. (2007). Public agencies and collaborative management approaches: Examining resistance among administrative professionals. *Administration & Society, 39*(5), 569–610. https://doi.org/10.1177/0095399707303635.

Powell, W. W. (1991). *Expanding the scope of institutional analysis.* Chicago: The university of Chicago Press.

Previtali, P., & Salvati, E. (2019). Social planning and local welfare. The experience of the Italian area social plan. *International Planning Studies, 24*(2), 180–194. https://doi.org/10.1080/13563475.2018.1528864.

Salvati, E. (2020). Riorganizzare il welfare locale. Il modello del governance network e l'esperienza dei Piani di Zona lombardi. *Studi Organizzativi, 1*, 67–92. https://doi.org/10.3280/SO2020-001003.

Saruis, T., Colombo, F., Barberis, E., & Kazepov, Y. (2019). Istituzioni del welfare e innovazione sociale: un rapporto conflittuale? *Italian Journal of Social Policy, 1*, 23–38.

Scharpf, F. W. (1988). The joint-decision trap: Lessons from German federalism and European integration. *Public Administration, 66*(3), 239–278. https://doi.org/10.1111/j.1467-9299.1988.tb00694.x.

Chapter 6
The Road towards the New Planning Phase (2021–2023) – Challenges and Opportunities

Abstract This conclusive chapter systematizes the findings of the book and opens a reflection on the immediate future of the next planning phase (2021–2023) and on the main shortcomings and problems that undermine the possibility to obtain more integration and coordination. Drawing from the theoretical and empirical evidence gathered in the book, this chapter reflects on some viable roads useful for the next planning phase in order to provide some answers to the organizational and policy-making dilemma of the Area Local Plan and local welfare.

Keywords Local area plan · Social policies · Welfare organization · Intermunicipal cooperation · Governance

6.1 A Complex Picture

Over the years, the Local Area Plans in the Lombardy region have undergone a considerable series of changes in their functions and aims. These changes are the result of large scale modifications in both the European and Italian systems of welfare (Madama 2019) and territorial decisions on the organisational and supply side dimensions of local welfare (Gori 2018; Salvati 2020). For the Local Area Plans these influences have resulted in their initial role as a resources/services provider being combined with that of being a central agent in the local welfare system, a *de facto* shifting of the bar of competence towards planning and the reduction of fragmentation in social assistance interventions. These changes have become inevitable both because of the evolution of citizens' needs in the social and healthcare fields and because of the various modifications in the governance of local welfare, the final form of which is represented by the reform of the socio-healthcare system in August 2015 (Regional Law No. 23/2015).

Above this, however, there is a national framework that over the last 20 years has helped to shift more and more powers and authority in the social and healthcare fields towards regional governments and local authorities. The regulatory field, in particular, has faced a substantial change of course: if the ambition of Law No. 328/2000 was to create a unified framework at state level for social policies

© The Author(s), under exclusive license to Springer Nature Switzerland AG 2021
P. Previtali, E. Salvati, *Local Welfare and the Organization of Social Services*,
https://doi.org/10.1007/978-3-030-66128-1_6

(improved access to services, concretisation of social rights, a greater participatory dimension in welfare) (Bifulco and Centemeri 2008), the subsequent reform of Title V of the Constitution in 2001, which strengthened the role of the Regions by giving them exclusive competence in the field of social policies and, the persistent absence of a definition for the Minimum Levels of Social Assistance (LIVEAS), have led instead to a framework of extreme fragmentation (Agostini 2008; Battistella et al. 2004; Previtali and Salvati 2019).

This fragmentation has also tended to be increased by the fact that the only holders of social functions are the municipalities, who therefore enjoy a very noticeable autonomy in this policy area. To all this, it should be added that in recent years there has been a rather constant reduction in the resources available to local authorities, despite the idea that it is precisely the local authorities that must develop a strategic and long-term approach to designing welfare policies. The Local Area Plans should therefore represent the governance formula of compromise between autonomy/territorialisation of policies and the containment of fragmentation.

We have seen that the theoretical framework that can valuably explain the adjustment and revision processes (incremental and medium-long term) that are reshaping the Lombardy region's local welfare and in particular the Local Area Plans functions is based on the following points:

(a) the need to review the welfare governance model and the actors/competencies involved (Andreotti and Mingione 2016);
(b) the implementation of policies more oriented to the mobilisation and activation of social resources than protection welfare models (Bifulco 2008). By activation we mean those policy processes that aim at strengthening social inclusion through policies on work, the fight against poverty and social support instruments, and are based on the principle of empowerment of the individual and the community (Geldof 1999; Bifulco 2008), thus moving towards a major "transversal and integrational approach" in the design of policies and measures;
(c) a greater attention towards social innovation as an instrument to define more up to date and needs adaptable policies (Moulaert 2013);
(d) the opportunity to define an organisational model able to collect and process social demands and provide affordable, innovative and effective policies (Busso and Negri 2012; Previtali and Salvati 2019).

The intersection of these different elements determines which answers to the requests and pressure for change and adaptation – as well as their degree of failure or success –covered by the umbrella concept of welfare territorialisation are most valuable (Kazepov 2010; Bifulco 2016). This framework fits, at least in part, within the neo-institutionalist perspective and the theory of organisation, an approach that aims to analyse the relationship and interaction between different aspects such as a given structure of institutions, actors, change and performance produced by actors and institutions (March and Olsen 1989; Busso and Negri 2012; DiMaggio and Powell 2000). This approach allows us to observe the endogenous factors and social constructions that influence institutions, and to study the structures, rules, and procedures (formal and informal) that define a given organisational structure. On the other hand, within this framework, the most mutable and varied aspects linked to the evolution of citizens' social needs and risks (Bonoli 2005), i.e. the target to which a given organisational and governance structure must respond, are included. Institutional isomorphism, governance structures, government connections, the relationship between stakeholders, the ways of responding to needs (and the definition of new needs) and performances are at the heart of this work.

Starting from this theoretical approach, throughout the book we have seen how Local Area Plans have become, over the years, the fulcrum of social policies at the local level, not only in terms of resources management/distribution but also for (among others) the planning and integration of policies. We aimed to provide a comprehensive framework for the analysis of this peculiar organisational model intended to enforce inter-municipal cooperation; an instrument useful for overcoming problems of agency loss, free riding and dedicated to strengthening coordination and mutual trust among actors. This kind of network is proving essential in a context of significant administrative fragmentation like the Italian one (Agostini 2008; Bertin and Carradore 2016; Madama 2019), as well as strategic for the planning of services in a leading sector like social assistance policies (Bonoli 2005).

6.2 Some Challenges and Critical Aspects

Despite these important elements, critical aspects are present and affect the effectiveness of this experience. Through an investigation of the Lombardy Region experience, we have tried to underline these problems and show how they relate to one another. Obviously, we are aware that this is only part of the picture, but we are confident that it will prove useful not only because the investigation used valid instruments for empirical analysis (in depth interviews, direct participation in working meetings, use of qualitative data, analysis of planning documents etc.) but also thanks to the definition of a theoretical framework which aims to shed light on almost all the elements that define the organisational arrangements of a Local Area Plan and its institutionalisation.

The first element worthy of attention, is the existence of a persistent sub-regional fragmentation that seems extremely hard to overcome, especially in a context of growing multilevel governance arrangements in the social assistance field too (Ferrera 2008; Kazepov 2010). Here the main issue is providing effective coordination among actors, resources (monetary and knowledge) and powers that are divided among different authority levels. Regional Decree No. 7631 partially attempted to reduce this fragmentation by proposing new governance models but, as we have seen, this attempt was far from successful.

Resistance to change from public administration (Oreg 2006; Kumar et al. 2007) and lack of mutual trust (Huxham 1991; Turrini et al. 2010; Previtali and Salvati 2019) seem to be useful proxies for exploring the failure of this kind of reform. This outcome opens room for further reflection. If administrative and political resistance is so strong when faced with forms of soft normative indications, then for regional governments three roads may be open:

1. to give up any effort of further governance coordination,
2. to embrace a hard strategy based on coercion and obligation,
3. to reflect on the opportunity to give more resources as a reward for aggregation strategies, stimulate broader inter-municipal cooperation through the definition of new territorial common policy goals and – in the Lombardy case – use the regional agencies like ATS to build new arrangements of governance in which the exchange, cooperation and coordination among actors is effectively pursued. But in this case, it means shifting the ATS (or ASL) responsibilities from those of governance to those of government, thereby giving them powers, authority and (more) autonomy over all the actors in the network.

Secondly, and directly connected to the first issue, a general difficulty in implementing a measure without obligation and/or administrative coercion is evident. While there has – probably – been general hostility from the Local Area Plans, who perceive this reorganisational proposal as excessively top down in its design/application, it is equally true that the monetary reward (limited in its amount) has not worked as a lever for governance change. On the other hand, it seems that the second part of the decree dedicated to the policy planning has worked better. This state of affairs can easily be explained by the fact that, despite the recognition – at different levels – that (a) the current regional Local Area Plan arrangements are too fragmented, and, (b) a significant number of Local Area Plans are not equipped to bear the weight of the new competencies due to their dimension/organisational structure, the public administration and political resistance to change is too strong to be scratched by soft law provisions.

Parochial attitudes, routinized behaviour, path dependence, compliance to changes as mere myth and ceremony, and difficulties in planning new organisational models are all elements that have severely affected the decree's chances of success.

The fragmentation issue, the need to plan new instruments to enforce coordination among all the actors of the network, a governance model better able to cope with new social challenges, a new way of managing fragmented resources and different policies/measures are – among others – elements that merit the attention of the regional policy maker and of all the territorial actors. For all these reasons the next 3 years of planning for the Local Area Plans, will be decisive and – desirably – will improve the valid intuitions of the 2015/2017 and 2018/2020 guidelines but overcome their limitations and shortcomings by approaching them with innovative ideas and courses of action.

6.3 Some Opportunities and Final Reflections

On the organisational side, Local Area Plans need to implement their action capacity by, for example, obtaining greater support from constitutive municipalities in terms of dedicated personnel. Above all it is essential that the planning capacity which is often frustrated by a public administration environment that is not always very keen to change or innovate (both in terms of goals and practices) is improved. In this case, the concrete risk is that of following a passive compliance to old and established rules (both formal and informal), and embracing a schematic and ordered approach to reality which could resemble a sort of iron cage trap (DiMaggio and Powell 2000; Ferrera 2020).

From this point of view it could be useful, as demonstrated by the literature (among others Thomson and Perry 2006; McGuire 2006; Kumar et al. 2007; Bifulco 2008), to stimulate dynamics of institutional reflexivity/adaptability and learning among administrative personnel and street level bureaucrats in order to support effective change within public administration and so create the conditions for revising critical aspects like that of fragmentation or lack of cooperation.

The input to proceed towards aggregation should probably be re-elaborated but not abandoned. Even though it was applied by few *areas*, Regional Decree No. 7631 did produce a positive reaction in some territories, which moved towards aggregations that differed in the organisational arrangements that were finally reached but that all had in common the consideration that small and not always well equipped Local Area Plans will in the future encounter more and more difficulties in the fulfilment of their planning mission and in their ability to provide answers to new and more complex social needs. This should encourage the policy maker to pursue new roads for the promotion of aggregation.

While these aggregations will obviously have to cope with problems concerning trust and collective action problems connected to the growing number of actors involved (Provan and Kenis 2008), they will also have the advantage of dealing with a narrower set of policies (the array of social policies), thereby reducing the transaction and coordination costs, which will theoretically be boosted by a social embeddedness supported by geographical proximity, sharing of similar tasks/goals and unavoidable exchanges between local government units which feed the opportunities for closer relationships (Tavares and Feiock 2018). At least theoretically, with a stronger and focused support, those kinds of aggregations would not be impossible to achieve. One of the main obstacles, that we have not been able to measure, could be the political responsiveness of local political leadership, concerning the pooling of resources and tasks with other local communities. But this problem should be easy to overcome, considering the advantage that is produced in terms of the efficiency and effectiveness of the services to deliver.

These general elements should be considered alongside the broader theme of governance in the sector of social and social-healthcare policies at the local level. The coordination among all the involved actors, the integration between the two policy sectors and the governance role effectively exercised by the ATSs as regional territorial agencies, are all rather weak. Here the real issue at stake is how to define an effective integrated system for social-healthcare supply; one able to take responsibility for the citizens by providing an integrated answer to needs that are – as shown, for example, through the analysis of the Local Area Plans' projects – multidimensional and multi sectorial, and involve different types of troubles, risks and fragilities. If the governance of the system is not really coordinated, nor based on a network of mutual trust, or collaboration and effective resource pooling, the unavoidable output will be an ineffective answer to citizens and a suboptimal model of collaboration among actors. A substantial help towards more integration could arrive from four connected actions that, at least partially, conceive also the role of the regional government:

1. reduction of policy fragmentation,
2. a broader and more integrated use of resources,
3. insistence on the enforcement of inter-municipal cooperation,
4. strong support for and encouragement of the planning capacity of the Local Area Plans.

The first point refers to the necessity of avoiding an "overproduction" of policy, a huge number of policies and actions that often overlap with national measures and that weigh on Local Area Plans, which in the end are responsible for implementing and/or acting as territorial gatekeepers for the distribution of benefits. A job that is often undertaken by human resources, who then have less time and resources to work on social planning and the realisation of established and new policies. This point is connected to the second, which is the management of funds. A proliferation of policies leads unavoidably to the fragmentation and parcelling of resources, that become more and more limited to specific projects and interventions, leaving a lesser degree of autonomy to the Local Area Plans. From this point of view it could be useful to start, at the regional level too, the planning of multi sectorial and integrated policies, based on a tighter exchange with the local level and also connected to a more proactive evaluation of outcomes. An evaluation model not simply based on the output or on the compliance with regional indications, but rather an evaluation of the whole policy cycle and its changing effects on the social landscape. For the purpose of a more effective planning, management and evaluation of social policy, an important element on which to push forward, both in continuity with the regional choices already made (the creation of the *Cartella Sociale Informatizzata*) and with a view to future planning, is the integrated management of data and knowledge tools. Local Area Plans need to have a greater flow of data and above all a close interconnection with other databases of other territorial authorities/actors. Such an effort extended to other territorial actors, could represent a decisive step towards stronger coordination and integration for the social supply network. This is related to an improvement in the services' digitalization, with the use of more advanced technological instruments both in the planning/management dimension of services and in the access/supply of social services.

Another critical element on which the regional government should continue to insist, also in light of the decree's indications, is the theme of quality and the appropriateness of services and policies, an issue that directly involves the Local Area Plans planning and supply. The insufficient attention paid by Local Area Plans to this issue, calls for a reflection on how the social supply system as a whole not only manages to intercept need, but how it effectively manages to offer a correct and appropriate response as well as quality in relation to the nature of the type of expressed need.

Moreover, it could be important to push forward in the direction of enforced aggregation. If the merge option resulted in a substantial failure in the absence of a strong normative bind/coercion, it would be interesting to pursue – at least – a soft model of governance reorganisation. In the future guidelines, a possible option could be support for a planning phase that – at least partially, some specific policies – could be located at the healthcare district level instead of within the single *local area plan*. This attempt could also represent a positive push for a more structured planning of integration between the social and healthcare sectors, which are still too loosely integrated compared to the nature of the expressed needs.

Finally support for the planning capacity of Local Area Plans should be considered a strategic priority. The analysis of the projects presented to qualify for the second reward step of the decree underline the existence of a mixed picture. Part of the Local Area Plans showed a consistent capacity in terms of project building and innovation in terms of social policies/actions planning, but a relevant group showed a surprising lack of ability. For this reason the regional government should reward those actors that are keen to change and innovate, while at the same time provide effective support for those who have difficulty in planning and project definition/delivery. This action could take different paths, starting from the concrete dissemination of good practices to the definition of shared moments of education and training; it should actively involve municipalities and Local Area Plans, and make clear to them that a new target should be the definition of innovative projects, which aim to break the path dependence of bureaucratisation and immobilism which characterises the design of social policies in some territories.

References

Agostini, C. (2008). Differenziazione e frammentazione territoriale delle politiche sociali. *Quaderni di Sociologia, 48*, 57–69. https://doi.org/10.4000/qds.833.

Andreotti, A., & Mingione, E. (2016). Local welfare systems in Europe and the economic crisis. *European Urban and Regional Studies, 23*(3), 252–266. https://doi.org/10.1177/0969776414557191.

Battistella, A., De Ambrogio, U., & Ranci Ortigosa, E. U. D. (2004). *Il piano di zona: costruzione, gestione, valutazione*. Roma: Carrocci.

Bertin, G., & Carradore, M. (2016). Differentiation of welfare regimes: The case of Italy. *International Journal of Social Welfare, 25*(2), 149–160. https://doi.org/10.1111/ijsw.12183.

Bifulco, L. (2008). Politiche pubbliche e partecipazione. Alcune piste per la comparazione fra Italia e Franca. *Rivista italiana di politiche pubbliche, 3*(2), 65–91. https://doi.org/10.1483/27437.

Bifulco, L. (2016). Citizenship and governance at a time of territorialization: The Italian local welfare between innovation and fragmentation. *European Urban and Regional Studies, 23*(4), 628–644. https://doi.org/10.1177/0969776414531969.

Bifulco, L., & Centemeri, L. (2008). Governance and participation in local welfare: The case of the Italian Piani di Zona. *Social Policy & Administration, 42*(3), 211–227. https://doi.org/10.1111/j.1467-9515.2007.00593.x.

Bonoli, G. (2005). The politics of the new social policies: Providing coverage against new social risks in mature welfare states. *Policy & Politics, 33*(3), 431–449. https://doi.org/10.1332/0305573054325765.

Busso, N., & Negri, N. (Eds.). (2012). *La programmazione sociale a livello zonale. Innovazione, tradizione, rituali.* Roma: Carocci.

DiMaggio, P. J., & Powell, W. W. (2000). The iron cage revisited institutional isomorphism and collective rationality in organizational fields. *Economics meets sociology in strategic management, 17,* 143–166. https://doi.org/10.1016/S0742-3322(00)17011-1.

Ferrera, M. (2008). Dal welfare state alle welfare regions: la riconfigurazione spaziale della protezione sociale in Europa. *La rivista delle politiche sociali, 3*(2008), 17–49.

Ferrera, M. (2020). Mass democracy, the welfare state and European integration: A neo-Weberian analysis. *European Journal of Social Theory, 23*(2), 165–183. https://doi.org/10.1177/1368431018779176.

Geldof, D. (1999). New activation policies: Promises and risks. *Linking welfare and work,* 13–26.

Gori, C. (Ed.). (2018). *Il welfare delle riforme? Le politiche lombarde tra norme ed attuazione.* Rimini: Maggioli.

Huxham, C. (1991). Facilitating collaboration: Issues in multi-organizational group decision support in voluntary, informal collaborative settings. *Journal of the Operational Research Society, 42*(12), 1037–1045. https://doi.org/10.1057/jors.1991.198.

Kazepov, Y. (Ed.). (2010). *Rescaling social policies: Towards multilevel governance in Europe.* Ashgate Publishing, Ltd..

Kumar, S., Kant, S., & Amburgey, T. L. (2007). Public agencies and collaborative management approaches: Examining resistance among administrative professionals. *Administration & Society, 39*(5), 569–610. https://doi.org/10.1177/0095399707303635.

Madama, I. (2019). La politica socioassistenziale. In M. Ferrera (Ed.), *Le politiche sociali.* Il Mulino: Bologna.

March, J., & Olsen, J. (1989). *Rediscovering institutions: The organizational basis of politics.* New York: Free Press.

Moulaert, F. (Ed.). (2013). *The international handbook on social innovation: Collective action, social learning and transdisciplinary research.* Edward Elgar Publishing.

Oreg, S. (2006). Personality, context, and resistance to organizational change. *European Journal of Work and Organizational Psychology, 15*(1), 73–101. https://doi.org/10.1080/13594320500451247.

Previtali, P., & Salvati, E. (2019). Social planning and local welfare. The experience of the Italian area social plan. *International Planning Studies, 24*(2), 180–194. https://doi.org/10.1080/13563475.2018.1528864.

Provan, K. G., & Kenis, P. (2008). Modes of network governance: Structure, management, and effectiveness. *Journal of Public Administration Research and Theory, 18*(2), 229–252. https://doi.org/10.1093/jopart/mum015.

Salvati, E. (2020). Riorganizzare il welfare locale. Il modello del governance network e l'esperienza dei Piani di Zona lombardi. *Studi Organizzativi, 1,* 67–92. https://doi.org/10.3280/SO2020-001003.

Tavares, A. F., & Feiock, R. C. (2018). Applying an institutional collective action framework to investigate intermunicipal cooperation in Europe. *Perspectives on Public Management and Governance, 1*(4), 299–316. https://doi.org/10.1093/ppmgov/gvx014.

Thomson, A. M., & Perry, J. L. (2006). Collaboration processes: Inside the black box. *Public Administration Review, 66,* 20–32. https://doi.org/10.1111/j.1540-6210.2006.00663.x.

Turrini, A., Cristofoli, D., Frosini, F., & Nasi, G. (2010). Networking literature about determinants of network effectiveness. *Public Administration, 88*(2), 528–550. https://doi.org/10.1111/j.1467-9299.2009.01791.x.

Index

CPSIA information can be obtained
at www.ICGtesting.com
Printed in the USA
LVHW010842190421
684886LV00002B/47